# SOCIAL PSYCHOLOGY

Longman Essential Psychology
Series editor: Andrew M. Colman

Other titles in this series:

# SOCIAL PSYCHOLOGY

EDITED BY

*Michael Argyle*
*and*
*Andrew M. Colman*

LONGMAN
London and New York

**Longman Group Limited**
Longman House, Burnt Mill
Harlow, Essex CM20 2JE, England
*and Associated Companies throughout the world.*


*Published in the United States of America
by Longman Publishing, New York*


© 1994 Routledge
This edition © 1995 Longman Group Limited
Compilation © 1995 Andrew Colman

This edition first published 1995

ISBN 0 582 27804X PPR

*British Library Cataloguing-in-Publication Data*
A catalogue record for this book is available from the British Library.

*Library of Congress Cataloging-in-Publication Data*
A catalogue record for this book is available from the Library of Congress.


Typeset by 25 in 10/12pt Times
Printed and bound by Bookcraft (Bath) Ltd

# CONTENTS

# NOTES ON EDITORS AND CONTRIBUTORS

MICHAEL ARGYLE is Emeritus Reader in Social Psychology at Oxford University, a fellow of Wolfson College, Oxford and Emeritus Professor at Oxford Brookes University. He has been Chairman of the Social Psychology section of the British Psychological Society and Visiting Professor at various universities in the United States, Canada, Australia, and elsewhere. He is the author of *The Psychology of Interpersonal Behaviour* (4th edn, 1983), *Bodily Communication* (2nd edn, 1988), *The Social Psychology of Work* (2nd edn, 1989), *The Social Psychology of Everyday Life* (1992), *Psychology and Social Class* and other books and papers.

RUPERT BROWN is Reader in Social Psychology at the University of Kent, Canterbury. He is editor of the European Monograph series in social psychology and the author of *Contact and Conflict in Intergroup Encounters* (1986) and *Group Processes: Dynamics Within and Between Groups* (1988).

PETER BULL is a Senior Lecturer in Psychology at the University of York, with special responsibility for teaching social psychology. He is a graduate both of Trinity College, Oxford, and of the University of Exeter, where he also obtained his PhD in psychology. He was elected a Fellow of the British Psychological Society in 1989. He is the author of *Body Movement and Interpersonal Communication* (1983), *Posture and Gesture* (1987) and (with Derek Roger) *Conversation: An Interdisciplinary Perspective* (1989).

ANDREW M. COLMAN is Reader in Psychology at the University of Leicester, having previously taught at Rhodes and Cape Town Universities in South Africa. He is the founder and former editor of the journal *Current Psychology* and Chief Examiner for the British Psychological Society's Qualifying Examination. His books include *Facts, Fallacies and Frauds in Psychology* (1987), *What is Psychology? The Inside Story* (2nd edn, 1988), and *Game Theory and its Applications in the Social and Biological Sciences* (2nd edn, 1995).

ALICE H. EAGLY obtained a doctorate in social psychology from the University of Michigan. She is Professor of Psychological Sciences at Purdue University, Indiana, USA. A past president of the Society for Personality and Social Psychology, she is a member of the editorial boards of several social psychology journals. She is the author of numerous articles and book chapters on attitudes as well as gender and sex differences. She is co-author (with Shelly Chaiken) of *The Psychology of Attitudes* (1993).

LESLEY FREDERIKSON has a BSc with a psychology major from Massey University, New Zealand, and a DPhil from the University of York, England. She was a Research Fellow for the New Zealand Federation of University Women from 1990 to 1992, studying the communication of information within doctor–patient interaction. She is currently a Research Fellow in the Psychology Department of Massey University studying the effects of post-traumatic stress disorder.

KLAUS JONAS took his doctorate in social psychology at the University of Tübingen, Germany. His current research concerns the prediction of health-related behaviours from social attitudes. He has published articles on health-related topics and on social stereotypes in the *European Journal of Social Psychology* and other journals.

DAVID J. SCHNEIDER is Professor of Psychology and Department Chair at Rice University, Houston, Texas. He obtained his PhD from Stanford University, California (1966) and has also taught at Amherst College, Brandeis University, Stanford University, Indiana University, and University of Texas at San Antonio. He is editor of the journal *Social Cognition*. He is the author of *Person Perception* (1979) and *Introduction to Social Psychology* (1988).

PETER B. SMITH is Reader in Social Psychology at the University of Sussex. His current interests are in cross-cultural studies in the fields of social and organizational psychology; he is associate editor of the *Journal of Cross-Cultural Psychology*. He is the author of *Groups Within Organisations* (1973) and *Group Processes and Personal Change* (1980), and co-author (with M. F. Peterson) of *Leadership, Organisations and Culture* (1988) and (with M. H. Bond) of *Social Psychology Across Cultures* (1993).

WOLFGANG STROEBE received a doctorate in experimental psychology from the University of Münster, Germany, and in social psychology from the London School of Economics. He has held academic positions in Britain, the United States, and Germany, and is now Professor at the University of Utrecht in The Netherlands. A past president of the European Association of Experimental Social Psychology and a member of the editorial boards of social psychology journals in the United States, Britain, and Germany, he has written numerous books and chapters on attitude change, group productivity, and health psychology. He is co-editor (with W. Meyer) of *Social Psychology and Economics* (1982); he is co-author (with M. S. Stroebe) of Bereavement and Health: The Psychological and Physical Consequences of Partner Loss (1987) and (with M. Hewson) of the *European Review of Social Psychology* (1992).

JAMES VIVIAN received his doctorate in social psychology at Boston College, Massachusetts, and is currently a research fellow in social psychology at the University of Kent, Canterbury. His current research is concerned with intergroup contact.

# SERIES EDITOR'S PREFACE

The *Longman Essential Psychology* series comprises twelve concise and inexpensive paperback volumes covering all of the major topics studied in undergraduate psychology degree courses. The series is intended chiefly for students of psychology and other subjects with psychology components, including medicine, nursing, sociology, social work, and education. Each volume contains five or six accessibly written chapters by acknowledged authorities in their fields, and each chapter includes a list of references and a small number of recommendations for further reading.

Most of the material was prepared originally for the Routledge *Companion Encyclopedia of Psychology* but with a view to later paperback subdivision – the contributors were asked to keep future textbook readers at the front of their minds. Additional material has been added for the paperback series: new co-editors have been recruited for nine of the volumes that deal with highly specialized topics, and each volume has a new introduction, a glossary of technical terms including a number of entries written specially for this edition, and a comprehensive new index.

I am grateful to my literary agents Sheila Watson and Amanda Little for clearing a path through difficult terrain towards the publication of this series, to Sarah Caro of Longman for her patient and efficient preparation of the series, to Brian Parkinson, David Stretch, and Susan Dye for useful advice and comments, and to Carolyn Preston for helping with the compilation of the glossaries.

ANDREW M. COLMAN

# INTRODUCTION

*Michael Argyle*
*University of Oxford, England*

*Andrew M. Colman*
*University of Leicester, England*

Social psychology is the study of social behaviour and the mental experience of people in social contexts. Many authorities view it as occupying the area between sociology on the one hand and individual psychology on the other. It includes the study of social interaction and communication, both verbal and non-verbal, behaviour in groups, social attitudes and persuasion, interpersonal attraction and social relationships, leadership and social influence, aggression and anger, altruism and helping behaviour, attribution and social cognition, bargaining and negotiation, conformity and social influence processes, cooperation and competition, group decision making, group dynamics, leadership and group performance, obedience to authority, prejudice and intergroup conflict, self-presentation and impression management, sex roles, sexual behaviour, social learning, and socialization. The chapters in this book deal with some of the most central and intensively studied topics in social psychology. In each case there has been a long history of research, from the "classical" early investigations onwards, there has been a lot of successful theoretical development, and there have been important applications. In each case there has been development of increasingly effective research methods, using better designs, more sophisticated statistics, and more realistic procedures. There has been some dispute among social psychologists over how relevant the results of artificial laboratory experiments are to everyday social life, and the reader will have to judge how far this problem has been solved in specific areas.

The birth date of social psychology is often given as 1908, when two influential early texts by McDougall (a psychologist) and Ross (a sociologist) were published, but the field did not really evolve a separate identity of its own until the mid-1930s and did not gain momentum until after the Second World War. The early development of social psychology was dominated by theories and research generated in the United States, although many of the most influential pioneers, including Fritz Heider and Kurt Lewin, were emigrants from Europe. After the foundation of the European Association of Experimental Social Psychology in 1967, pressure began to build towards reducing the global dominnnce of American social psychology. European social psychology has maintained the American tradition of experimental research but has also tended to give more prominence to non-experimental approaches, such as discourse analysis, social representations research, and various qualitative methods.

Chapter 1, by Klaus Jonas, Alice H. Eagly, and Wolfgang Stroebe, is about attitudes and persuasion, including the nature of attitudes, their relation to behaviour, and how to change them. Political, religious, racial, commercial, and other attitudes are of great practical importance, and many individuals and organizations are naturally interested in trying to influence them. Attitudes were conceived by early researchers as combinations of beliefs, affects, and behaviours. The first step was to measure them, and this was successfully achieved. Then a serious problem emerged – attitudes often failed to predict behaviour at all well. It was soon found that one of the main reasons for this was that behaviour is influenced by social pressures as well as by attitudes; the joint effect of the two was incorporated by Füshbein and Ajzen in the mid-1970s into an influential theory in which weights are attached to attitudes and to social norms. There has been much useful criticism and elaboration of this model, including the observation that behaviour is often more spontaneous and less rational than the model assumes, and that intentions do not always lead to behaviour.

Many theories have been put forward to predict attitude change; those based on learning theory imply that conditioning or reinforcement is sufficient, whereas cognitive theories imply that there have to be changes in thinking about the topic, which may be brought about by persuasive argument. It is often supposed that behaviour can be manipulated by changing the incentives for different choices; but this does not always work, and especially during the 1960s and 1970s cognitive dissonance theory explored some of the paradoxical reversals that can occur. Other theories focus on the effects of different kinds of arguments, and in 1986 Petty and Cacioppo proposed an influential theory according to which there are two basic kinds of persuasion, one route through the quality of the argument itself, the other through peripheral cues such as the alleged expertise of the source.

For more information on the psychology of attitudes, see Eagly and Chaiken (1993). This topic has practical implications, for example for the design of campaigns for better health behaviour. These are found to be more effective if there is personal contact, and this leads us to the topic of face-to-face influence, which is discussed in the next chapter.

Chapter 2, by Peter B. Smith, is about social influence processes, and it presents the current state of our knowledge about some classic issues in social psychology. One of the earliest questions was about the effect of the mere presence of a second person working at a task, like pulling in a tug-of-war. Usually they pull harder, and this is called *social facilitation*, but under some conditions they make less effort − there is "social loafing". When several individuals make a collective decision, they often make a more extreme (or riskier) one than when alone. This has been called the *group polarization* (or *risky shift*), and there are various theories for it. Conformity is the tendency of members of groups to go along with the majority view, and this has been studied in experiments from the classic studies of Solomon Asch in the early 1950s onwards. An important development came in France in the mid-1970s from Serge Moscovici, who found evidence for a different kind of influence from persistent minorities in groups. Obedience has been another classic problem, first investigated by Stanley Milgram at Yale University in the early 1960s.

The study of leadership has had a long history, and we know that certain styles of leadership are more effective than others. At higher levels of leadership "charismatic" leaders have been found to be particularly effective. However, the optimal style varies with circumstances (the "contingencies"), and it is also realized that leadership is really a relationship and that there is influence in both directions. Furthermore, leaders have to maintain successful relations with their own superiors and colleagues as well as with their subordinates.

Social influence can be exerted in several different ways, using rewards, punishment, or expertise, for example; in informal settings such as door-to-door sales, there are a number of influence methods, such as the "foot-in-the-door" technique, that have been studied experimentally. Further information on social influence can be found in Cialdini (1993); on leadership and groups at work in Argyle (1989), and on social interaction in general in Argyle (1994).

Chapter 3, by David J. Schneider, is on attribution and social cognition. Much recent research in social psychology has been about how people perceive and interpret social events; this is important because it affects how they will behave towards the people concerned. The earliest work was on perception of others' emotional states and forming impressions of their personalities. There are a number of interesting issues here, such as how we integrate different information about others, and how we use implicit theories about the way personalities fit together.

Observers may attribute the behaviour of others either to their personality or to the situation, and this leads to several common errors and biases. For example, depressed patients tend to blame themselves for bad things that happen to them, and under-achievers tend to think that their failure is due to lack of ability rather than lack of effort, with the result that they do not try as hard as they might.

Cognitive social psychology is about how we process information about social phenomena, and it relates social psychology to more basic cognitive processes. We use knowledge structures or *schemas*, as Frederick Bartlett called them, and make inferences that may be wrong by using various short cuts or *cognitive heuristics*. Our memory too is selective and biased. Further reading on social cognition can be found in the massive two-volume *Handbook of Social Cognition* edited by Wyer and Srull (1994), and applications of attribution theory are discussed by Myers (1993).

In chapter 4, James Vivian and Rupert Brown discuss prejudice and intergroup conflict − among the world's most pressing problems. Can social psychology help to resolve conflicts between groups? One of the first major research efforts identified the *authoritarian personality* as the kind of individual who is most likely to be prejudiced. This can account for individual differences but not for variations in hostile attitudes over time or in different places. Another idea was that we dislike those who are different from ourselves, especially if they have different beliefs; there is evidence for this too, but also some contradictory evidence. Prejudice has been shown to be related to frustration, for example in lynchings in the United States, and also to *relative deprivation* (believing that one is worse off that other individuals or groups).

Prejudice is accompanied by stereotypes − unfavourable beliefs about other groups. Out-groups tend to be seen as more homogeneous than the ingroup, and the negative ideas may be due to *illusory correlations*, for example between skin colour and crime, and by the stereotypes maintained through cognitive processes such as selective memory.

During the 1960s, Muzafer Sherif and his colleagues showed that realistic conflict could cause hostility between groups − groups of small boys at least − and could be resolved by cooperation towards shared goals. However, attempts to use this idea on a larger scale have not worked very well. Henri Tajfel's *social identity theory* proposed that the basis of prejudice is the enhancement of self-esteem by discrimination against out-groups, and this has led to a lot of interesting research, though not many real-life applications. According to the *contact hypothesis*, sheer social contact is the best way to reduce prejudice, as happened successfully in mixed black and white regiments in the United States army, but unfortunately it does not always work. There are certain optimal conditions for it to do so. These were embodied in the "jig-saw classroom", which involved equal-status cooperation in small ethnically mixed groups, and in experiments where "pleasant and typical" members of another group were encountered. Further reading on inter-group conflict and how it can be reduced can be found in Myers (1993).

Chapter 5, by Peter Bull and Lesley Frederikson, is about non-verbal communication (NVC). This is a relatively new field, in which British researchers have been especially active. Laboratory experiments have been very successful in this field, and there are theoretical links with neurology and evolutionary theory on one side, and with anthropology and linguistics on the other. This chapter starts with the intriguing question of how far non-verbal signals are sent or received without conscious awareness. One of the most important roles of NVC is the expression and communication of emotional states, and here the work of Paul Ekman and his colleagues has been very influential. They found six emotional states that are expressed in the face in the same way in different cultures, though expressions are sometimes suppressed by *display rules* that vary from one culture to the next; where this fails there can be non-verbal "leakage" of the true state. Facial expression is the main channel for expression of emotions, but tone of voice is also important.

There is a quite different kind of NVC during speech, to supplement the purely verbal content of what is being said, to manage turn-taking, and to provide feedback from listeners. This is done by gestures, shifts of gaze, and changes in vocal quality. Another role of NVC is in the management of relationships with others; in courtship, for example, postural congruence is an indicator of rapport. There are interesting individual differences; those between the NVC of men and women are reviewed here, and there are tests for accuracy of perception of NVC. The main practical application of this kind of research has been in social skills training, for patients, for doctors and other professionals, and in assertiveness training, for example. Other aspects of non-verbal communication are described in Argyle (1988) and Knapp (1992).

Readers who wish to pursue any of the topics of this volume in greater depth should consult the recommendations for further reading at the end of each chapter and perhaps also the additional readings mentioned in this introduction. This slim volume does not cover the whole of social psychology, but there are chapters on social psychology in other books in the Longman Essential Psychology series. The main ones are as follows. John Lazarus's chapter on "Behavioural Ecology and Evolution" in *Biological Aspects of Behaviour* (Kimble and Colman, 1995) presents the sociobiology, that is, the evolutionary explanation, of cooperation and altruism, parenting, and mate choice; Willem J. M. Levelt's chapter on "Psycholinguistics" in *Cognitive Psychology* (French and Coleman, 1995) deals with conversation, has more on non-verbal communication, and also discusses sign language; Michael Argyle's chapter on "Social Skills" in *Learning and Skills* (Mackintosh and Colman, 1995) describes how competent social behaviour is performed, which skills are most effective, and how people can be trained to be more socially effective; Russell G. Geen's chapter on "Social Motivation" in *Emotion and Motivation* (Parkinson and Colman 1995) goes further into the arousing effect of the presence of others and into the important topics of self-presentation and social anxiety; Sarah E. Hampson's chapter on "The Construction of Personality" in *Individual Differences and Personality* (Hampson and Colman, 1995) discusses personality in the eyes of others, and as constructed by the self, to make a self-image; Peter K. Smith's chapter on "Social Development" in *Developmental Psychology* (Bryant and Colman, 1995) is about the origins of social behaviour in childhood and the social behaviour and relationships of children, including friendship, aggression and leadership; and John Weinman's chapter on "Health Psychology" in *Controversies in Psychology* (Colman, 1995) deals with a topic that has become one of the main fields of application of social psychology, especially the effects of social support, beliefs about health, and the skills of professionals.

## REFERENCES

Argyle, M. (1988). *Bodily communication* (2nd edn.). London: Methuen.
Argyle, M. (1989). *The social psychology of work* (2nd edn.). London: Penguin.
Argyle, M. (1994). *The psychology of interpersonal behaviour* (5th edn.). London: Penguin.
Bryant, P. E., & Colman, A. M. (eds) (1995). *Developmental psychology*. London and New York: Longman Group Limited, Ch. 3.
Colman, A. M. (ed.) (1995). *Controversies in Psychology*. London and New York: Longman Group Limited Ch. 5.
Cialdini, R. B. (1993). *Influence: Science and practice* (3rd edn.). New York: HarperCollins.
Eagly, A. H., & Chaiken, S. (1993). *The psychology of attitudes*. Fort Worth, TX: Harcourt Brace Jovanovich.
French, C. C., & Colman, A. M. (eds) (1995). *Cognitive psychology*. London and New York: Longman Group Limited, Ch. 3.
Hampson, S. E., & Colman, A. M. (eds) (1995). *Individual differences and personality*. London and New York: Longman Group Limited, Ch. 2.
Kimble, D., & Colman, A. M. (eds) (1995). *Biological aspects of behaviour*. London and New York: Longman Group Limited, Ch. 2.
Knapp, M. L. (1992). *Nonverbal communication in human interaction* (3rd edn.). Fort Worth, TX: Harcourt Brace Jovanovich.
Mackintosh, N. J., & Colman A. M. (eds) (1995). *Learning and skills*. London and New York: Longman Group Limited, Ch. 5.
Myers, D. G. (1993). *Social psychology*. New York: McGraw-Hill.
Parkinson, B., & Colman, A. M. (eds) (1995). *Emotion and motivation*, London and New York: Longman Group Limited, Ch. 3.
Wyer, R. S., & Srull, T. K. (eds) (1994). *Handbook of social cognition* (2 vols). Hillsdale, NJ: Lawrence Erlbaum Associates.

# ATTITUDES AND PERSUASION

## Klaus Jonas
### Universität Tübingen, Germany
## Alice H. Eagly
### Purdue University, Indiana, USA
## Wolfgang Stroebe
### Rijksuniversiteit te Utrecht, The Netherlands

The campaign against smoking, an exceptionally effective persuasion campaign, began in 1964 with the publication of the report of the United States Surgeon-General's Advisory Committee on Smoking and Health (1964). Persuasive materials carried by the media emphasized the unhealthy consequences of smoking, and compulsory health warnings were introduced on tobacco advertisements and cigarette packages. Increases in excise taxes on tobacco made smoking considerably more expensive. Largely as a result of this anti-smoking campaign, smoking is no longer perceived as glamorous, but as a health risk and an addiction. Moreover, especially in the USA, smoking has declined substantially.

This chapter examines some of the psychological processes involved in effective persuasion campaigns. The first part of the chapter introduces the concepts of attitude, belief, and behaviour, and analyses the relations between them. The second part focuses on two general strategies of persuasion – namely, the use of rewards or incentives to change attitudes and the use of persuasive argumentation.

## ATTITUDES, BELIEFS, AND BEHAVIOURS

### The concept of attitude

*Attitude* may be defined as a psychological tendency to evaluate a particular entity with some degree of favour or disfavour (see Eagly & Chaiken, 1993; Zanna & Rempel, 1988). For example, one might have an attitude towards reducing agricultural subsidies in the European Community. The entity towards which people hold an attitude (e.g., reducing agricultural subsidies) is called an *attitude object*. Anything that is discriminable or is an object of thought can be evaluated and therefore can function as an attitude object. Examples of attitude objects thus include people, one's own behaviour (e.g., smoking), concrete objects like one's car, and more abstract entities like social policies and ideologies. Attitudes may be positive or negative and differ in their extremity as well.

People can express their attitudes in various ways, through their cognitions, affects, and behaviours. *Cognitions* refer to the thoughts, or beliefs, that a person has about the attitude object; a belief is any perceived link between an attitude object and an attribute. *Affects* refer to the feelings, moods, emotions, or sympathetic nervous system activity that a person experiences in relation to an attitude object. *Behaviours* refer to a person's overt actions with respect to the attitude object and include intentions to behave that are not necessarily expressed in action. In general, a person's cognitions, affects, and behaviours are positive (i.e., have favourable implications for the attitude object) to the extent that the person holds a positive attitude and are negative (i.e., have unfavourable implications for the object) to the extent that the person holds a negative attitude.

2

## Relations between attitudes and beliefs

Several algebraic models attempt to describe precisely the relation between attitudes and beliefs. Among these approaches is Fishbein and Ajzen's (1975) expectancy-value model, which assumes that one's attitude is a function of one's beliefs when these beliefs are represented as the sum of the expected values of the attributes one ascribes to the attitude object. According to this approach, each attribute has an expectancy and a value attached to it. The *expectancy* is the individual's subjective probability that the attitude is characterized by the attribute, and the *value* is the individual's evaluation of the attribute. For example, a person may have a definite expectancy (high subjective probability) that *European integration* (attitude object) will contribute to *political stability in Europe* (positively evaluated attribute). To predict an attitude from such beliefs, the expectancy and value terms associated with each attribute are multiplied together, and these products are added (see Equation 1). By this approach, people should hold positive attitudes towards things that they think have good attributes and negative attitudes towards things that they think have bad attributes.

$$\text{Attitude} = \Sigma \text{ Expectancy} \times \text{Value} \tag{1}$$

Despite the success of this model, its implicit assumption that people form attitudes by summing a number of attributes of the attitude object has been questioned. Sometimes people may proceed more efficiently by taking into account only one or a very few attributes of the attitude object (e.g., McGuire, 1985), or they may form attitudes based on their affective responding or their behaviours rather than their beliefs.

## Relation between attitudes and behaviours

If attitudes influence overt behaviour, people with positive attitudes towards a given attitude object should engage in behaviours that approach, support, or enhance it, and those with negative attitudes should engage in behaviours that avoid, oppose, or hinder the object. However reasonable it may seem that attitudes should be related to behaviours in this way, considerable controversy surrounds the ability of attitudes to predict behaviour. Central in this debate was Wicker's (1969) review of 42 studies of the attitude-behaviour relation, which found an average correlation of only about .15 and led him to conclude that attitudes are typically unrelated or only slightly related to overt behaviours. Although Wicker's and other critics' conclusions were initially accepted by many social scientists, important principles by which attitude-behaviour correlations can be increased were subsequently set forth.

From a psychometric perspective, much of the variation in attitude-behaviour correlations can be understood in terms of the *reliability* and *validity* of an investigator's measures of behaviour. A single instance of behaviour is an unreliable indicator of an attitude because the performance of the behaviour depends upon many factors in addition to the attitude. For example, whether an environmentalist places used bottles into a recycling bin during a particular week may depend not only on his or her attitude towards environmental preservation but also on factors like opportunity, time, or resources. Yet when a number of somewhat unreliable behavioural indicators of an attitude are aggregated into a composite behavioural index, the non-attitudinal factors that influence the single behaviours should tend to cancel one another. Because such a composite behavioural measure should more reliably reflect the underlying attitude, it should show a higher correlation with attitude. This *aggregation principle*, initially proposed by Fishbein and Ajzen (1974), has been effectively demonstrated in a number of studies.

A single behavioural observation may be not only an unreliable measure of attitude, but also a relatively invalid measure because it embodies specific features that are not incorporated into the attitude that the social scientist has chosen to study. As Ajzen and Fishbein (1977) pointed out, each single behaviour incorporates (1) a specific *action*, (2) directed at a *target*, (3) in a *context*, (4) at a *time* or occasion. In contrast, many of the most commonly studied attitudes indicate only the target of an attitude (e.g., one's attitude towards a healthy lifestyle is an "attitude towards a target"). Such general attitudes can be expressed by a variety of specific actions performed in a variety of contexts and times. For example, an individual's positive attitude towards a healthy lifestyle can be manifested in a wide range of actions such as jogging, eating a balanced diet, giving up smoking, and reducing consumption of alcoholic beverages; these actions can be performed in a variety of contexts and times. To be a maximally valid indicator of attitude towards a healthy lifestyle, a composite index of behaviours should consist of a representative sample of all the behaviours that are relevant to this attitude. Yet the range of relevant behaviours would be much narrower for a more narrowly formulated attitude such as attitude towards jogging before breakfast each morning. In general, correlations between attitudes and behaviours increase to the extent that the two measures are defined at the same level of generality in terms of their action, target, context, and time elements (see Ajzen & Fishbein, 1977). Ajzen (1988) has labelled this generalization the *principle of compatibility*.

## Attitudinal models of behaviour

### Expectancy-value models

Fishbein and Ajzen (1975) proposed a theory for predicting behaviour from attitude and other variables. The type of attitude considered by this theory is attitude towards one's own behaviour (e.g., one's attitude towards voting in favour of a particular political party or candidate). This *theory of reasoned action*, which is restricted to the prediction of volitional or voluntary behaviours, assumes that the proximal cause of a behaviour is one's intention to engage in it. Intention represents motivation to perform a behaviour in the sense of the individual's conscious plan to exert effort to carry out the behaviour. Intention to engage in a behaviour is itself a function of the person's attitude towards engaging in the behaviour, and her or his perception of the extent to which significant others think that she or he should engage in the behaviour. This latter component is called *subjective norm*. This model can be stated algebraically as follows:

$$B(f)BI = w_1 A_B + w_2 SN. \tag{2}$$

In this equation $B$ refers to behaviour, $BI$ to behavioural intention, $A_B$ to attitude towards the behaviour, and $SN$ to subjective norm; $w_1$ and $w_2$ are empirical weights indicating the relative importance of the attitudinal and normative components. Attitude towards the behaviour ($A_B$) is itself a function of one's beliefs about the perceived consequences of the act multiplied by the evaluation of each consequence (i.e , a form of Equation 1). Subjective norm is a function of one's perceptions of other people's preferences about whether one should engage in the particular behaviour (weighted by one's motivation to comply with these perceived preferences).

The theory of reasoned action has been tested in numerous studies of quite diverse behaviours, including voting, weight loss, consumer behaviour, and family planning behaviour (Ajzen & Fishbein, 1980). According to a meta-analysis of this research (Sheppard, Hartwick, & Warshaw, 1988), the theory has been well supported. Specifically, the mean correlation in the studies reviewed in the meta-analysis was .66 for the prediction of intention from attitude and subjective norm. For the relation between intention and behaviour, the mean correlation was .53.

Among the criticisms of the theory of reasoned action is the view that limiting the model to volitional behaviours excludes actions that one cannot engage in merely by deciding to do them. Behaviours such as having a party, for example, require resources, cooperation, and specialized skills (Liska, 1984). Also challenged was the reasoned-action assumption that attitude and subjective norm are sufficient proximal causes of intentions. To circumvent these criticisms, many revisions of the theory have been proposed, all of which retain as their central feature the ideas that people form attitudes towards behavioural acts by scrutinizing the consequences of acts and that these attitudes then impact indirectly or directly on behaviour. Best known among these variant models is Ajzen's (e.g., 1988, 1991) *theory of planned behaviour*. This model, which is designed to predict non-volitional as well as volitional behaviours, adds to the reasoned action model a new predictor of intention (and behaviour) labelled *perceived behavioural control*, which is defined as one's perception of how easy or difficult it is to perform the behaviour. Perceived control is in turn a function of the individual's beliefs about how likely it is that he or she possesses the resources and opportunities required to execute the behaviour. Research has shown that the addition of this variable can often improve the prediction of intention and behaviour; yet models adding a variety of other variables have also improved prediction under certain circumstances (see Eagly & Chaiken, 1993).

## Spontaneous processing model

The models of behaviour discussed so far conceive of people as rational decision-makers who form behavioural intentions by thinking about the consequences of future actions. Although these models do not imply that individuals have to weigh all the possible consequences of behavioural alternatives before they act, their assumption that actions are controlled by intentions suggests that behaviour presupposes some deliberative cognitive processing. However, as Fazio (1990) argued, such deliberative thinking occurs only when individuals are able and willing to think about their future actions. People are more likely to expend cognitive effort on such thinking if important outcomes are involved and if they have the time and peace of mind to deliberate. When outcomes are unimportant or when there is little opportunity to deliberate, attitudes might affect behaviour through a more spontaneous process.

Fazio (1986, 1990) reasoned that such spontaneous behaviour is influenced, not by the attitudes towards behaviours considered in the expectancy-value tradition, but by more general attitudes – that is, attitudes towards the entities or targets towards which behaviours are directed. For example, one's attitude towards a particular brand of breakfast cereal, rather than one's attitude towards *purchasing* this cereal on a particular trip to the store, might determine whether one purchases it.

From Fazio's perspective, attitudes are associations between the attitude object and an evaluation. The sequence that links an attitude to behaviour is initiated when the attitude is accessed from memory. The likelihood that the attitude is spontaneously activated when a person observes an attitude object (or a cue associated with it) is a function of the *accessibility*, or ease of recall, of the attitude. Accessibility depends, in turn, on the strength of the individual's mental association between the attitude object and her or his evaluation of the object. Repeated activation of the link between the attitude object and its evaluation strengthens the association. To the extent that this association is strong, the evaluation is accessed easily and quickly in response to cues conveyed by the attitude object. According to Fazio, only attitudes with high associative strength have a high probability of spontaneous (and automatic) activation. Once such an attitude is activated, it instigates attitude-congruent perceptions of the attitude object (i.e., positive

6

perceptions if the attitude is positive and negative perceptions if it is negative), and these perceptions in turn evoke attitude-congruent behaviour.

Consistent with Fazio's (1986) theory, higher accessibility (operationalized by the speed with which an attitude-relevant cue elicits an evaluative response) is related to higher attitude-behaviour consistency. Moreover, accessibility may account for the influence of several variables on the magnitude of attitude-behaviour correlations. For example, the reason why attitudes based on direct experience are better predictors of behaviour than attitudes based on indirect experience may be that they are more accessible from memory (see Fazio, 1986).

In conclusion, contemporary psychologists have provided two approaches to understanding the psychological processes by which attitudes affect behaviour. The first approach consists of a family of expectancy-value models that treat attitudes towards behaviours as causes of behaviours and regard the perceived consequences of behaviour as determinants of these attitudes. The second approach predicts behaviour from more general attitudes and emphasizes that attitudes that are more accessible from memory are more likely to direct behaviour.

## STRATEGIES OF PERSUASION

Webster's (1986) unabridged dictionary defines "to persuade" as "to induce by argument, entreaty, or expostulation into some mental position" or "to win over by an appeal to one's reason and feelings" (p. 1687). Although the term *persuasion* thus focuses on argumentation, as the Latin root of the word would suggest, a broader interpretation of the term would encompass other forms of social influence such as the use of incentives and rewards. Reflecting such breadth, our discussion focuses on persuasion through the use of rewards or incentives as well as argument-based persuasion.

### Reward- and incentive-based persuasion

The study of incentive-based persuasion concerns the extent to which attitudes and behaviour can be influenced by rewards and punishments. Early theorists generally believed that attitudinal responses are automatically strengthened by their immediate consequences through processes of *classical* and *instrumental* conditioning (e.g., Lott & Lott, 1968; Staats & Staats, 1958; Verplanck, 1955). However, with the emergence of cognitive theories of social learning (e.g., Bandura, 1986), psychologists began to emphasize the *informative* and *incentive* functions of reinforcements.

### *Classical conditioning of attitudes*

Through classical conditioning a stimulus that is initially incapable of

7

eliciting a particular response (the conditioned stimulus) acquires the ability to do so through repeated association with a stimulus that already evoked this response (the unconditioned stimulus). In Pavlov's (1927) classic experiment on dogs, a tone that was presented repeatedly just prior to food eventually elicited salivation, a response previously evoked only by the food.

Instead of using food as an unconditioned stimulus, Staats and Staats (1958) used words that elicited positive affect (e.g., *vacation*, *gift*) or negative affect (e.g., *bitter*, *failure*). These words were presented auditorially to subjects immediately after the visual presentation of the name of a nationality in what was apparently a learning experiment. For half of the subjects, Dutch was consistently paired with positive adjectives and Swedish with negative adjectives; for the other half, the pairing was reversed. The presentation of other nationalities consistently paired with neutral words was intended to disguise the purpose of the experiment. When the target nationalities were later rated on an evaluative scale, the nationality that had been associated with positive words was rated more positively than the nationality paired with negative words. Interpreting their findings in terms of automatic conditioning processes, Staats and Staats reasoned that the positive or negative reaction initially evoked by the adjectives had been passed on to the nationality name by mere association.

The conditioning processes modelled by experiments of this type may have important implications for understanding the development of prejudice, because social groups (e.g., national or racial groups) are often systematically associated with negative information in the media. Classical conditioning may also offer an explanation for the effectiveness of advertising practices that pair brand names with positive but seemingly irrelevant stimuli (e.g., a photograph of a handsome man or beautiful scenery).

## Instrumental or operant conditioning of attitudes

Consistent with Skinner's (1957) assertion that human verbal behaviour is subject to the same operant conditioning principles that govern much animal learning, numerous studies during the late 1950s and 1960s investigated the instrumental, or operant, conditioning of people's attitudinal statements and other verbal behaviour. Whereas in classical conditioning the organism has no control over the reaction that is originally elicited by the unconditioned stimulus and later by the conditioned stimulus, in operant conditioning the organism must produce a response first, before it can be strengthened or weakened by differential reinforcement.

Studies of instrumental conditioning of attitudes typically used a question-and-answer format in which the experimenter queried subjects about their attitudes towards some issue and then reinforced responses in a particular attitudinal direction. For example, in one early study, subjects were interviewed by telephone about the educational policy of their university

(Hildum & Brown, 1956). The telephone caller verbally reinforced some subjects by responding with "good" whenever their responses implied a favourable attitude towards university policy, and other subjects were reinforced for answers implying a negative attitude. Consistent with predictions, subjects reinforced for positive attitudes increasingly agreed with favourable statements, whereas the trend was reversed for subjects reinforced for negative attitudes.

### Role of cognition in conditioning processes

Interpretations of classical and instrumental conditioning of attitudes in terms of behaviourist theories which assume that conditioning is an automatic, affective process were challenged by cognitively oriented psychologists who argued that conditioning processes are based on learning the contingencies, or relationships between events, that characterize the conditioning experiment. According to cognitive reinterpretations of classical conditioning of attitudes, subjects in these studies typically recognize the systematic relationship between the adjectives and the nationality names. They may then merely respond to the demands of the experimental situation by telling the experimenter what they think she or he wants to hear (e.g., Page, 1969), or they may form beliefs about these nationalities on the basis of the information conveyed by the adjectives (e.g., Fishbein & Ajzen, 1975).

Similarly, cognitive reinterpretations of instrumental conditioning of attitudes assume that subjects typically become aware of the contingency between their responses and the receipt of reinforcement. For example, Insko and Cialdini (1969) suggested that the interviewer's "good" response has two consequences: first, it informs subjects of the attitudinal position held by the interviewer, and second, it establishes positive rapport between subjects and interviewers. Subjects' friendly feelings towards the interviewer then motivate them to conform to the interviewer's attitude.

Although behaviourist and cognitive interpretations of conditioning were hotly debated during the 1970s, this controversy has never been resolved. Existing empirical evidence does not rule out the possibility that attitudinal conditioning may sometimes influence attitudes without mediation by higher-order cognitive processes (see Eagly & Chaiken, 1993).

### Incentive-induced attitude change

Consistent with the expectancy-value models of behaviour presented earlier in the chapter are the attempts of powerful institutions such as governments to change the "costs" of a given behaviour through monetary incentives, taxation, or legal sanctions. For example, by increasing taxes on tobacco and alcoholic beverages, governments have had some success in inhibiting unhealthy behaviours such as smoking and drinking excessive alcohol (see

Moore & Gerstein, 1981; Novotny, Romano, Davis, & Mills, 1992). Like the demand for most commodities, the demand for alcoholic beverages and cigarettes responds to changes in price, and increases in price result in decreased sales of alcoholic beverages (e.g., Johnson & Oksanen, 1977) and cigarettes (e.g., Walsh & Gordon, 1986). Moreover, evidence for the successful use of legal sanctions to discourage risky behaviours comes from studies demonstrating the considerable impact of laws mandating the use of seat-belts (e.g., Fhanér & Hane, 1979).

Limiting this approach is the tendency for changes in the "price" of a given behaviour to influence mainly the attitude towards purchasing the product or service that enables one to engage in the behaviour. Consistent with the assumption that attitude towards a behaviour reflects the perceived consequences of the behaviour, one's attitude towards *buying* alcoholic beverages might become more negative, given the price constraints, whereas one's attitude towards the critical behaviour itself (i.e., *drinking* alcoholic beverages) might remain positive. Consequently, although a marked increase in the price of alcoholic beverages is likely to induce people to buy fewer alcoholic beverages, they might drink at their old level of consumption when the price constraints are not in effect (e.g., when drinks are freely available at a party).

Despite the narrow impact of such incentive-based programmes, under certain conditions incentive-induced behaviour change could produce more general attitude change. Consider, for example, the use of positive incentives to induce individuals to engage in behaviours for which they have negative expectations. Should these expectations be *unrealistically* negative, their experience with the behaviour would allow them to view it more positively. Also, communicators can imply that rewards would follow, not from behaviour change, but from broader changes in attitudes and beliefs (see Hovland, Janis, & Kelley, 1953).

Attitude change is also likely when individuals are induced to engage in a behaviour that is *discrepant* from their attitudes. There is evidence from research conducted in the cognitive dissonance tradition (Festinger, 1957) that under certain conditions engaging in attitude-discrepant behaviour to gain some reward or avoid some penalty produces a negative state of arousal known as *cognitive dissonance*. In order to reduce this aversive state, people may change their attitude in the direction of greater consistency with their behaviour. According to cognitive dissonance theory, dissonance should be greater when the reward for the attitude-discrepant behaviour is *small* rather than large, because the lack of external justification for engaging in the behaviour increases the dissonance that follows from the behaviour's inconsistency with the attitude.

This negative relation between the size of a reward and the amount of attitude change induced by attitude-discrepant behaviour was demonstrated in a classic study by Festinger and Carlsmith (1959) and has been frequently replicated in subsequent research (see Eagly & Chaiken, 1993). However, subsequent research also uncovered a number of limiting conditions. Specifically, the negative relation between the magnitude of reward and the amount of attitude change occurs only when subjects feel free to refuse to engage in the attitude-discrepant behaviour and when this behaviour has negative consequences either for themselves or for other people.

Finally, offering incentives for the performance of a particular behaviour can result in a more negative attitude towards this behaviour. This so-called *overjustification effect* is likely to occur when people are rewarded for engaging in a behaviour that they already find intrinsically interesting and pleasurable (e.g., Lepper, Greene, & Nisbett, 1973). The positive attitude towards the behaviour is undermined by the positive incentives, perhaps in part because people attribute their behaviour to the incentives rather than to their intrinsic interest in the behaviour (see Bem, 1972).

In conclusion, both attitudes and behaviours may be changed through incentives and rewards. Yet the psychological processes by which these effects may occur are diverse and include classical and operant conditioning, the learning of contingencies, the reduction of cognitive dissonance, and the attribution of one's behaviour to external rewards and costs.

### Argument-based persuasion

The study of argument-based persuasion concerns the extent to which people's attitudes, beliefs, and behaviour are changed by relatively complex information consisting of a verbal communication or message. Research in this area has traditionally been oriented to understanding the categories of variables highlighted by Lasswell's (1948, p. 37) classic question, "Who says what in which channel to whom with what effect?" *Who* thus refers to the characteristics of the communicator or message source, *what* refers to the content of the message, *in which channel* refers t · the medium through which the message is communicated, *to whom* refers to the characteristics of the recipients of the message, and *with what effect* refers to the nature of the changes that the message produces. Research in this area has not produced "laws of persuasion" in the form of general relationships between particular independent variables and amount of persuasion. Instead, relations involving a particular independent variable typically interact with other variables. For example, communicator credibility or communicator likability, two of Lasswell's "who-variables", generally have a positive impact on the persuasiveness of a message, but this effect is much stronger under some circumstances than others and is sometimes absent or even reversed from its usual direction.

To make sense out of such phenomena, psychologists have produced theories of persuasion that illuminate the psychological processes that are relevant to persuasion and take into account the circumstances under which each process is likely to be important. This process-theory approach to understanding persuasion began with the work carried out at Yale University under the direction of Carl Hovland (Hovland et al., 1953).

Subsequent decades have witnessed increasingly complex theories of persuasion that have illuminated more and more of the relations observed in the thousands of persuasion experiments that have appeared in the empirical literature (see Eagly & Chaiken, 1993; Petty & Cacioppo, 1986a). In these experiments, subjects usually receive a relatively complex verbal message containing a number of arguments that support an overall position on an issue. Subjects give their responses, ordinarily on questionnaires designed to assess, in addition to change in attitudes and beliefs, a number of the mediating processes that may underlie their tendencies to change or resist changing.

## Theories of systematic processing

Some persuasion theories have emphasized what might be termed systematic processing by highlighting the importance of message recipients' detailed processing of message content. This approach began with Hovland et al.'s (1953) suggestion that the impact of persuasive communications can be understood in terms of a sequence of processes — attention to the message, comprehension of its content, and acceptance of its conclusions. By this approach, independent variables that influence persuasion act not only directly on people's tendencies to accept the messages' conclusions, but also indirectly through their impact on two causally prior processes, attention and comprehension. Persuasion could fail to occur because of omissions in any of these three information-processing phases: recipients could fail to attend to the message, fail to comprehend its content, or fail to accept what they have comprehended. Persuasion variables such as the inclusion of vivid or pallid imagery in persuasive argumentation might have their impact through any of these processes. For example, vivid imagery might attract attention, yet distract recipients from comprehending message content, or directly facilitate acceptance of the information.

### Information-processing model

McGuire (e.g., 1972) proposed a longer chain of processes that are relevant to persuasion: presentation, attention, comprehension, yielding (or acceptance), retention, and behaviour. This perspective assumes that after exposure to the message, recipients must pay attention to it in order for attitude change to be produced. Subsequently, the overall position it advocates and the arguments provided to support this position must be comprehended. Also, recipients must yield to, or agree with, the message content they have comprehended if any attitude change is to be detected. If this change is to persist over a period of time, recipients must retain their changed attitudes.

Finally, if impact is to be observed, recipients must behave on the basis of their changed attitudes. McGuire argued that the failure of any of these steps to occur causes the sequence of processes to be broken, with the consequence that the subsequent steps do not occur.

Empirical work relevant to McGuire's model has emphasized in particular the mediating role of the two steps involving reception of message content: attention to the message and comprehension of its content. Reception of message content should in general facilitate persuasion, at least under the ordinary circumstances in which the message contains cogent persuasive arguments. Moreover, many independent variables may act simultaneously on reception of message content and yielding to it. For example, message recipients' intelligence may facilitate their ability to comprehend messages but reduce the likelihood that they would yield to them. Because the relative importance of these two processes would depend on the nature of the situation, the model makes a number of predictions. Concerning recipients' intelligence, for example, the model predicts that more intelligent recipients will be more persuaded than less intelligent recipients by complex, well-argued messages for which the positive relation between intelligence and message reception should be the primary determinant of persuasion. In contrast, less intelligent recipients will be more persuaded than more intelligent recipients by simple, poorly argued messages for which the negative relation between intelligence and yielding to the message should be the primary determinant of persuasion. Such predictions have received moderately good support (see Eagly & Chaiken, 1993; Rhodes & Wood, 1992).

## Cognitive-response model

Also illustrating the systematic approach to understanding persuasion is the cognitive-response model initially proposed by Greenwald (1968) and developed by several social psychologists (see Petty, Ostrom, & Brock, 1981). This perspective reflects the general proposition that people's attitudes are a function of the cognitions that they generate about the objects of their attitudes. This approach thus emphasizes the mediating role of the idiosyncratic thoughts or "cognitive responses" that message recipients generate as they receive and reflect on persuasive communications. Messages should be persuasive to the extent that they evoke favourable thoughts and unpersuasive to the extent that they evoke unfavourable thoughts. Moreover, these effects of the favourability of recipients' thoughts should be magnified to the extent that they engage in extensive message-relevant thinking.

This cognitive-response perspective produced numerous persuasion experiments, each of which manipulated a variable that impacted on extent of message processing (e.g., distraction, message repetition, issue involvement) and crossed this variable with a single other variable – namely, the quality of the arguments given by the message, a factor that reliably affects the favourability of recipients' message-relevant thoughts. The general pattern of findings in these cognitive-response experiments is well known: the favourability of recipients' thoughts (as controlled by argument quality) determines persuasion only to the extent that recipients process the message relatively thoroughly and therefore react to the quality of the arguments. For example, distraction, a variable that can disrupt recipients' abilities to think about message content, has differing impact, depending on the quality of the arguments contained in the message. With high-quality messages that elicit predominantly favourable thoughts, distraction should inhibit these favourable thoughts and therefore inhibit persuasion; with low-quality messages that elicit predominantly unfavourable thoughts, distraction should inhibit these unfavourable thoughts and therefore facilitate persuasion. Petty, Wells, and Brock (1976) confirmed these hypotheses in an early cognitive-response experiment. Although quite a few additional persuasion variables have been investigated within this tradition, the theory none the less is relevant mainly to those variables that are clearly related to message recipients' abilities or motivation to engage in message-relevant thinking.

## Dual-process theories

Subsequent persuasion theories took on a broader mission than the systematic processing theories did. Whereas the systematic theories had emphasized message reception and cognitive elaboration of persuasive argumentation, the newer theories consider in addition the idea that people adopt attitudes on bases other than their understanding and evaluation of the semantic content of persuasive argumentation. This general dual-process approach has gained considerably in popularity in recent years. Among dual-process theories are the elaboration likelihood model (Petty & Cacioppo, 1986a, 1986b), which incorporates a peripheral route to persuasion, and the heuristic-systematic model (Chaiken, 1980; Chaiken, Liberman, & Eagly, 1989), which considers simple decision rules or heuristics that mediate persuasion. These theories emphasize contrasting modes of processing and trade at least in part on the idea borrowed from cognitive psychology that cognitive processing can be carried out at a superficial or deeper level. Following the general notion that people process information superficially and minimally unless they are motivated to do otherwise, these attitude theories thus stress that message recipients must have sufficient motivation to turn to more effortful, systematic forms of processing persuasive communications. They must also have the capacity to engage in this more deliberative form of processing.

In the elaboration likelihood model, Petty and Cacioppo (1986a, 1986b) postulated a *central route to persuasion*, which they identified primarily with the message-relevant thinking that served as the mediating process in the cognitive response approach. They postulated in addition *a peripheral route to persuasion*, which they conceptualized quite broadly as the product of any of a variety of mechanisms that cause persuasion in the absence of scrutiny of persuasive arguments. The peripheral route would thus encompass cognitive mechanisms such as heuristic decision rules and attributional reasoning, affective mechanisms such as classical and operant conditioning, and social relational mechanisms such as maintaining role relationships and favourable self-identities. The principal idea of the elaboration likelihood model is that message recipients follow the central route when situational and individual difference variables ensure high motivation and ability for issue-relevant thinking (i.e., when elaboration likelihood is high); they follow the peripheral route when motivation or ability (or both) are low (i.e., when elaboration likelihood is low).

This perspective has led to a range of interesting predictions. Prototypical predictions are that when elaboration likelihood is high, persuasion is influenced by the quality of persuasive arguments, but when elaboration likelihood is low, persuasion is influenced by peripheral cues, which are variables capable of affecting persuasion without influencing recipients' scrutiny of the arguments contained in messages. Illustrating this approach is Petty, Cacioppo, and Goldman's (1981) study in which source expertise functioned as a peripheral cue. Subjects listened to a message advocating senior comprehensive exams, a policy the university was ostensibly considering for the following year (establishing "high personal relevance", which should induce high motivation to think about the message) or the following decade (establishing "low personal relevance", which should induce little motivation to think about the message). Subjects were exposed to either high-quality or very low-quality arguments favouring this recommendation, and the message was said to be based on a report prepared by either a local high school class (low source expertise) or the "Carnegie Commission on Higher Education" (high source expertise). As predicted, the results showed that in the low relevance conditions, source expertise influenced subjects' attitudes and argument quality did not, whereas in the high relevance conditions source expertise had no impact on attitude whereas argument quality did.

The heuristic-systematic model also postulates two mediational paths to persuasion (Chaiken, 1980; Chaiken, Liberman, & Eagly, 1989). This theory's concept of systematic processing resembles central processing in the elaboration likelihood model. In contrast, heuristic processing is more narrowly formulated than peripheral processing because it focuses on simple decision rules that message recipients use to judge the validity of messages. For example, as a consequence of invoking the simple rule that "experts' statements can be trusted", message recipients may agree more with expert than inexpert communicators without having fully absorbed or evaluated the semantic content of the argumentation contained in a message. Because heuristic processing is associated with a particular type of psychological mechanism, this conceptualization has produced several unique hypotheses regarding the persuasive impact of communication variables that serve as heuristic cues. In particular, the model's assumption that heuristics are learned knowledge structures has suggested several cognitive principles that govern their operation and therefore their impact on persuasion. Specifically, these heuristics must be available (i.e., stored in memory for potential use) and accessible (i.e., activated or accessed from memory) in order to influence persuasion. In addition, cognitive heuristics vary in their strength or perceived reliability; more reliable heuristics have more judgmental impact than less reliable heuristics. These principles have suggested novel mechanisms by which certain variables may influence persuasion.

In conclusion, social psychologists have provided several theories of argument-based persuasion and have conducted extensive research to test these models. The earlier theories emphasized the systematic processing of message content, whereas later theories added the assumption that people are often not sufficiently motivated to engage in message-relevant thinking and therefore base their decision to accept or reject a persuasive message on heuristic cues or other peripheral processes. These newer theories have allowed investigators to cast a much wider net among independent variables and to make effective predictions about the conditions under which these variables influence persuasion.

## IMPLICATIONS FOR THE DESIGN OF PERSUASION CAMPAIGNS

In applications of the research discussed in this chapter for the design of persuasion campaigns, one issue to consider is whether the target audience has the capacity and motivation to engage in detailed processing of the arguments employed in the communication. If people lack the ability or motivation to comprehend, scrutinise, and evaluate the content of the communication, it is futile to expend great effort on developing a thoughtful, detailed argumentation. Instead, one should rely on mechanisms that do not depend on argumentation for their effectiveness. One could use classical conditioning, heuristic processing, and other mechanisms to influence the audience. It is no coincidence that most of the well-known advertisements for cigarettes, perfumes, or sunglasses rely heavily on this peripheral route to persuasion. If it can be assumed that members of the target audience are both motivated and able to assess the validity of more complex argumentation, it is advisable to develop a thoughtful and coherent argumentation that can stand up to this kind of scrutiny. Thus, the campaign against cigarette smoking made ample use of the scientific evidence on the health consequences of smoking.

Even if a communicator manages to produce the desired attitude change, this impact will not necessarily be translated into behaviour change. As we discussed earlier, there are many reasons why people might not act in accord with their attitudes. With communications urging preventive health behaviours, one of the main problems is that individuals usually have to give

16

up some pleasurable activity (or engage in some unpleasant activity) in the here and now to avoid some negative consequences that might occur at a much later time. One way to bridge this time gap is the introduction of costs that are immediately effective; examples include imposing price increases or instituting legal restrictions and penalties.

The war against smoking was not fought only with arguments and scientific evidence. Increases in the price of cigarettes and legal restrictions on smoking made a significant contribution to the reduction in levels of smoking. Also, knowledge that smoking in enclosed environments endangers the health of others created strong social pressures against smoking (i.e., a subjective norm that countered smoking). This multi-process approach was no doubt essential to the striking success of the anti-smoking campaign.

## FURTHER READING

Ajzen, I. (1988). *Attitudes, personality, and behavior*. Milton Keynes: Open University Press.

Eagly, A. H., & Chaiken, S. (1993). *The psychology of attitudes*. Forth Worth, TX: Harcourt Brace Jovanovich.

Fazio, R. H. (1990). Multiple processes by which attitudes guide behavior: The MODE model as an integrative framework. In M. P. Zanna (Ed.) *Advances in experimental social psychology* (vol. 23, pp. 75–109). San Diego, CA: Academic Press.

Petty, R. E., & Cacioppo, J. T. (1986). The elaboration likelihood model of persuasion. In L. Berkowitz (Ed.) *Advances in experimental social psychology* (vol. 19, pp. 123–205). San Diego, CA: Academic Press.

## REFERENCES

Ajzen, I. (1988). *Attitudes personality, and behavior*. Milton Keynes: Open University Press.

Ajzen, I. (1991). The theory of planned behavior. *Organizational Behavior and Human Decision Processes, 50*, 179–211.

Ajzen, I., & Fishbein, M. (1977). Attitude–behavior relations: A theoretical analysis and review of empirical research. *Psychological Bulletin, 84*, 888–918.

Ajzen, I., & Fishbein, M. (1980). *Understanding attitudes and predicting social behavior*. Englewood Cliffs, NJ: Prentice-Hall.

Bandura, A. (1986). *Social foundations of thought and action: A social cognitive theory*. Englewood Cliffs, NJ: Prentice-Hall.

Bem, D. J. (1972). Self-perception theory. In L. Berkowitz (Ed.) *Advances in experimental social psychology* (vol. 6, pp. 1–62). San Diego, CA: Academic Press.

Chaiken, S. (1980). Heuristic versus systematic information processing and the use of source versus message cues in persuasion. *Journal of Personality and Social Psychology, 39*, 752–766.

Chaiken, S., Liberman, A., & Eagly, A. H. (1989). Heuristic and systematic processing within and beyond the persuasion context. In J. S. Uleman & J. A. Bargh (Eds) *Unintended thought* (pp. 212–252). New York: Guilford.

Eagly, A. H., & Chaiken, S. (1993). *The psychology of attitudes*. Fort Worth, TX: Harcourt Brace Jovanovich.

Fazio, R. H. (1986). How do attitudes guide behavior? In R. M. Sorrentino & E. T. Higgins (Eds) *Handbook of motivation and cognition: Foundations of social behavior* (pp. 204–243). New York: Guilford.

Fazio, R. H. (1990). Multiple processes by which attitudes guide behavior: The MODE model as an integrative framework. In M. P. Zanna (Ed.) *Advances in experimental social psychology* (vol. 23, pp. 75–109). San Diego, CA: Academic Press.

Festinger, L. (1957). *A theory of cognitive dissonance*. Evanston, IL: Row, Peterson.

Festinger, L., & Carlsmith, J. M. (1959). Cognitive consequences of forced compliance. *Journal of Abnormal and Social Psychology*, *58*, 203–210.

Fhanér, G., & Hane, M. (1979). Seat belts: Opinion effects of law-induced use. *Journal of Applied Psychology*, *64*, 205–212.

Fishbein, M., & Ajzen, I. (1974). Attitudes toward objects as predictors of single and multiple behavioral criteria. *Psychological Review*, *81*, 59–74.

Fishbein, M., & Ajzen, I. (1975). *Belief, attitude, intention and behavior: An introduction to theory and research*. Reading, MA: Addison-Wesley.

Greenwald, A. G. (1968). Cognitive learning, cognitive response to persuasion, and attitude change. In A. G. Greenwald, T. C. Brock, & T. M. Ostrom (Eds) *Psychological foundations of attitudes* (pp. 147–170). San Diego, CA: Academic Press.

Hildum, D. C., & Brown, R. W. (1956). Verbal reinforcement and interviewer bias. *Journal of Abnormal and Social Psychology*, *53*, 108–111.

Hovland, C. I., Janis, I. L., & Kelley, H. H. (1953). *Communication and persuasion: Psychological studies of opinion change*. New Haven, CT: Yale University Press.

Insko, C. A., & Cialdini, R. B. (1969). A test of three interpretations of attitudinal verbal reinforcement. *Journal of Personality and Social Psychology*, *12*, 333–341.

Johnson, J. A., & Oksanen, E. H. (1977). Estimation of demand for alcoholic beverages in Canada from pooled time series and cross sections. *Review of Economics and Statistics*, *59*, 113–118.

Lasswell, H. D. (1948). The structure and function of communication in society. In L. Bryson (Ed.) *The communication of ideas: Religion and civilization series* (pp. 37–51). New York: Harper & Row.

Lepper, M. R., Greene, D., & Nisbett, R. E. (1973). Undermining children's intrinsic interest with extrinsic reward: A test of the "overjustification" hypothesis. *Journal of Personality and Social Psychology*, *28*, 129–137.

Liska, A. E. (1984). A critical examination of the causal structure of the Fishbein/Ajzen attitude-behavior model. *Social Psychology Quarterly*, *47*, 61–74.

Lott, A. J., & Lott, B. E. (1968). A learning theory approach to interpersonal attitudes. In A. G. Greenwald, T. C. Brock, & T. M. Ostrom (Eds) *Psychological foundations of attitudes* (pp. 67–88). San Diego, CA: Academic Press.

McGuire, W. J. (1972). Attitude change: The information-processing paradigm. In C. G. McClintock (Ed.) *Experimental social psychology* (pp. 108–141). New York: Holt, Rinehart & Winston.

McGuire, W. J. (1985). Attitudes and attitude change. In G. Lindzey & E. Aronson (Eds) *Handbook of social psychology* (3rd edn, vol. 2, pp. 233–346). New York: Random House.

Moore, M. H., & Gerstein, D. R. (1981). *Alcohol and public policy: Beyond the shadow of prohibition*. Washington, DC: National Academy Press.

Novotny, T. E., Romano, R. A., Davis, R. M., & Mills, S. L. (1992). The public health practice of tobacco control: Lessons learned and directions for the States in the 1990s. *Annual Review of Public Health*, *13*, 287–318.

18

Page, M. M. (1969). Social psychology of a classical conditioning of attitudes experiment. *Journal of Personality and Social Psychology, 11*, 177–186.

Pavlov, I. P. (1927). *Conditioned reflexes: An investigation of the physiological activity of the cerebral cortex.* New York: Oxford University Press.

Petty, R. E., & Cacioppo, J. T. (1986a). *Communication and persuasion: Central and peripheral routes to attitude change.* New York: Springer-Verlag.

Petty, R. E., & Cacioppo, J. T. (1986b). The elaboration likelihood model of persuasion. In L. Berkowitz (Ed.) *Advances in experimental social psychology* (vol. 19, pp. 123–205). San Diego, CA: Academic Press.

Petty, R. E., Cacioppo, J. T., & Goldman, R. (1981). Personal involvement as a determinant of argument-based persuasion. *Journal of Personality and Social Psychology, 41*, 847–855.

Petty, R. E., Ostrom, T. M. & Brock, T. C. (Eds) (1981). *Cognitive responses in persuasion.* Hillsdale, NJ: Lawrence Erlbaum.

Petty, R. E., Wells, G. L., & Brock, T. C. (1976). Distraction can enhance or reduce yielding to propaganda: Thought disruption versus effort justification. *Journal of Personality and Social Psychology, 34*, 874–884.

Rhodes, N., & Wood, W. (1992). Self-esteem and intelligence affect influenceability: The mediating role of message reception. *Psychological Bulletin, 111*, 156–171.

Sheppard, B. H., Hartwick, J., & Warshaw, P. R. (1988). The theory of reasoned action: A meta-analysis of past research with recommendations for modifications and future research. *Journal of Consumer Research, 15*, 325–343.

Skinner, B. F. (1957). *Verbal behavior.* New York: Appleton-Century-Crofts.

Staats, A. W., & Staats, C. K. (1958). Attitudes established by classical conditioning. *Journal of Abnormal and Social Psychology, 57*, 37–40.

United States Surgeon-General's Advisory Committee on Smoking and Health (1964). *Smoking and health: Report of the Advisory Committee of the Surgeon General of the Public Health Service.* Princeton, NJ: Van Nostrand.

Verplanck, W. S. (1955). The control of the content of conversation: Reinforcement of statements of opinion. *Journal of Abnormal and Social Psychology, 51*, 668–676.

Walsh, D. C., & Gordon, N. P. (1986). Legal approaches to smoking deterrence. *Annual Review of Public Health, 7*, 127–149.

*Webster's Third New International Dictionary of the English Language Unabridged* (1986). Springfield, MA: Merriam-Webster.

Wicker, A. W. (1969). Attitude versus actions: The relationship of verbal and overt behavioral responses to attitude objects. *Journal of Social Issues, 25*(4), 41–78.

Zanna, M. P., & Rempel, J. K. (1988). Attitudes: A new look at an old concept. In D. Bar-Tal & A. W. Kruglanski (Eds) *The social psychology of knowledge* (pp. 315–334). Cambridge: Cambridge University Press.

# 2

# SOCIAL INFLUENCE PROCESSES

## Peter B. Smith
### University of Sussex, England

| | |
|---|---|
| **Social facilitation effects** | **Classification of social influence** |
| **Conformity** | **strategies** |
| **Minority influence** | **Social influence in informal** |
| **Leadership** | **settings** |
|   Obedience | **Charisma** |
|   Leadership style | **Social influence as negotiation** |
|   Contingency theories | **Further reading** |
|   Rethinking the question: what | **References** |
|     is leadership | |

Most of the subject matter of social psychology could be said to be concerned with the way in which we influence the perceptions and the actions of one another. However, research into social psychology during the twentieth century has become increasingly focused into a series of discrete research areas whose interconnections are insufficiently explored. In this way, we have reached the point where two books on social influence by social psychologists (Cialdini, 1988; Turner, 1991) have virtually no shared content.

Studies of social influence divide most readily between those that consider how the mere presence of other people influences one's behaviour, and those that focus on situations where people actively try to influence one another. The first of these two areas has been most typically known as social facilitation, but includes the related effects referred to as the risky shift, group polarization, and social loafing. The second type of study has addressed phenomena such as leadership, obedience, persuasion, conformity, and minority influence.

## SOCIAL FACILITATION EFFECTS

The very first social psychological experiment was undertaken in the 1880s by a French engineering professor named Ringelmann (Kravitz & Martin, 1986). He showed that the more members there were in a tug-of-war team, the less hard each member of the team pulled. Numerous other experiments have confirmed that while on some tasks the presence of others does indeed inhibit performance, on others performance is actually enhanced. Zajonc (1965) proposed that these mixed results may be explained by the proposition that the presence of others influences us to perform better on familiar tasks and worse on unfamiliar ones. This attempt at integration has proved difficult to test, since a task that is familiar to one person may well be unfamiliar to others.

A later series of studies has focused on some of the tasks where the presence of others does seem to inhibit performance, and promotes what Latané, Williams, and Harkins (1979) have dubbed "social loafing". Latané's thinking was based on the observation that bystanders become less likely to come to the aid of those in distress if there are others at hand. He devised a series of experimental tasks (for instance clapping or shouting as loudly as possible, alone or in the presence of others), which did consistently elicit social loafing, in a very similar manner to Ringelmann's original tug-of-war studies. Loud clapping and shouting are not on the whole a widespread activity of individuals on their own, but they are quite frequent in crowds. Zajonc's theory is therefore not much help in explaining social loafing. However, a number of other factors have been found to reduce or eliminate social loafing. For instance, Brickner, Ostrom and Harkins (1986) showed that social loafing occurred only where subjects thought that the task was unimportant and that no one else was watching their performance. When tasks with more everyday plausibility have been used, it has been found in more group-oriented countries such as China and Japan that social loafing effects are not merely eliminated but actually reversed. Here, the presence of others is found to enhance performance on the same tasks where a social loafing effect is found in more individualistic western countries (Smith & Bond, 1993). Evidently social facilitation is a function not only of the type of task, but also of the type of relationship existing between the individual, the group they are part of, and any other audience there may be.

These same issues have come to the fore in discussions of what is now known as group polarization. This is an effect occurring when experimental subjects are asked to make a series of group decisions on topics where they have already recorded individual preferences. It is reliably found that the group's decision will be more extreme, in one direction or the other, than the average of the individual group members' choices. Initially it was thought that the phenomenon occurred only with decisions involving risk, and that group decisions were more in favour of risk than was the average of individual decisions. The effect thus became known for a time as the 'risky shift' (Stoner, 1961). However, it was subsequently found that on some decisions the group decision moves toward caution rather than risk, and that the polarization effect occurred on decisions that did not involve risk at all.

Numerous explanations of this effect have been proposed, and it appears that two of them have some validity (Brown, 1986). First, the additional time available to a group to reach their decisions after individual judgements have been made provides opportunities for members to exchange information on what choices others have made. If we presume that there is a socially desirable position that each group member would like to take up, then the exchange of information will reveal to some members that their initial choices are less desirable than they thought. When the topic involves risk and is one on which members would like to be seen as bold and adventurous, those who chose cautiously will move their choice toward risk. On topics where members would rather be seen as prudent and cautious, members who chose the riskiest options will move toward caution. Thus the mere exchange of information about who chose what can induce polarization.

A second explanation of polarization is also tenable (Brown, 1986). In discussion, group members may point out relevant information that others have missed and they may argue persuasively for its importance. Analyses of transcripts of group discussions show that this does occur.

Turner (1991) argues that, in addition to these explanations, polarized decisions are reached because group members wish to define their identity more positively and distinctively, in contrast to members of other groups whom they might expect to take up more average positions. Polarization does indeed become more extreme when groups are informed of the presumed decisions of other groups relevant to them (Doise, 1969).

Although the polarization effect has been of considerable interest to social psychologists, it is of limited practical importance, since it is found in groups where members have not met before and where no group leader is appointed. Where members do already know one another (Semin & Glendon, 1973), or where there is an established leader (Jesuino, 1986), polarization is not always found, and other types of social influence can be presumed to be more potent. Juries do, however, provide a practical instance in which polarization effects are likely to occur.

The interest aroused by the polarization studies most probably occurred because the effect that was found did not concur with the common-sense expectation that groups would make decisions that were close to the average of individuals' views. Had they done so, it would have been considered as an instance of conformity. It may well be that despite the different outcome of polarization studies, polarization and conformity are both explicable in similar ways. In order to consider this possibility we must now examine conformity studies.

## CONFORMITY

Conformity is said to occur when group members move their opinions or behaviour towards that of the group's majority view, or else if uniformity already exists within a group. The classic study in this field was that of Asch (1951), who asked subjects to say which of several lines matched the length of a set of stimulus lines that he provided. Asch's experimental accomplices were also asked to make the judgements; although the task was easy, they gave the wrong response on about two-thirds of the trials. An example of one of the sets of lines used is shown in Figure 1. It was found that on around one-third of the crucial trials the experimental subject conformed to the erroneous majority.

It is by no means certain that this type of experiment captures the essence of conformity pressures in everyday social settings. One's judgements of aspects of the physical world such as line lengths may be governed by different factors than are the endorsement of particular attitudes or beliefs. For instance Allen and Levine (1968) showed that when judgements were asked for about matters of belief (such as the population of the United States), the presence of one judge giving correct answers did not inhibit some conformity toward the erroneous majority. In contrast, within the Asch experiments, even one accomplice responding correctly eliminates all conformity to the erroneous majority.

Despite these limitations on the validity of the Asch design, it has proved highly influential, and replications of the effect found have been widely published. Deutsch and Gerard (1955) proposed that there were two elements explaining the Asch effect, which they termed informational and normative social influence. Informational influence occurs in situations of ambiguity, where a person in doubt is likely to use others' responses as guideposts as to what is going on. Normative influence occurs in situations where a person wishes to give a good impression to others, or to avoid some type of sanction. The interviews conducted by Asch with his subjects indicated that both explanations were plausible. Some subjects denied that they had been aware of

*Figure 1*   An example of the Asch line judgement task: which of the lines on the right matches the one on the left?

giving incorrect responses – they had unwittingly used others as marker posts. But other subjects conceded that they had indeed given wrong responses, but had done so for fear of embarrassment from being out of line with everyone else's judgements.

The Asch experiments are frequently misinterpreted. As Friend, Rafferty, and Bramel (1990) point out, Asch actually found that on two-thirds of the judgements his subjects successfully resisted conformity pressures. At least in the case of judgements of unambiguous stimuli, conformity is thus the exception rather than the rule. However, Deutsch and Gerard were able to show that by introducing variations in experimental design, conformity rates would rise and fall in ways that they could predict. For instance, where a team prize was offered for correct responses, conformity rose, presumably because normative pressures were increased.

The explanations for conformity advanced by Deutsch and Gerard are rather similar to some of those put forward by investigators of group polarization. In both cases the exchange of information appears important as does the need of group members to present themselves in ways that gain social approval. Turner's reformulation of the polarization effect in terms of relations between groups rather than just within groups was touched on earlier. Abrams, Wetherell, Cochrane, Hogg, and Turner (1990) show that similar processes can also affect the rates of conformity in Asch-type conformity experiments. They found that information given to subjects as to who were the experimental accomplices giving the false answers made a good deal of difference to conformity rates. The accomplices were always described as fellow-students at a neighbouring prestigious university. However, when they were also stated to be students of psychology, conformity was high, whereas when they were described as students of ancient history, conformity was much lower. As Abrams and colleagues point out, there is no reason to expect that students of history would be any less able to judge line lengths than are students of psychology. The different conformity rates must be attributed to the fact that fellow-students of psychology were seen as more closely linked to the subjects and therefore as a group to which they would want to conform.

The misinterpretation of Asch's findings as showing that members of groups always conform to the majority has also been challenged by another group of researchers, based primarily in France. They argue that under certain circumstances influence may also be exerted by minorities within groups.

## MINORITY INFLUENCE

Moscovici (1976) made a re-analysis of Asch's results, and succeeded in showing that conformity rates varied widely depending on the *proportion* of trials on which the accomplices had given incorrect answers. He concluded that in deciding whether or not to conform, subjects were paying attention to the *consistency* of others' judgements. From this point he went on to consider whether we might be influenced by those who made consistent judgements, regardless of whether they were a majority of group members or a minority.

Moscovici then conducted a series of experiments designed to illustrate how group minorities can, over time, change the views of the majority, by giving consistent responses. For instance in a colour judging task, a minority were instructed to consistently describe a blue-green colour as green. It was found that the views of majority subjects as to where the boundary might be drawn between the colours considered to be blue and those considered to be green was moved and that the effect persisted even when further judgements were required after the minority had withdrawn.

Moscovici (1980) subsequently developed his theory further to assert that the manner in which majorities and minorities achieve their influence differs. He proposes that majorities impose their views through a direct process of requiring compliance. On the other hand, minorities achieve their effect more indirectly, but they achieve a more lasting conversion of the majorities' views rather than mere overt compliance.

Findings in favour of minority influence have not always proved replicable, but this may be because Moscovici's complex and provocative hypotheses have several components. For instance, some studies have found that minorities do achieve influence, but only when they are willing to compromise, rather than adopting the consistently deviant position advocated in the original theory (e.g., Nemeth, Swedlund, & Kanki, 1974). It has also been repeatedly shown that the influence achieved by the minority depends on who they are. If they are identified as being similar to members of the majority, they are much more influential than if they differ by, for instance age, gender, or social category (Clark & Maass, 1988).

The studies of minority influence thus show that it is achieved not so much by a particular style of behaviour in the group, but more by a combination of attributes and behaviours that lead others to take note of their views. Whether such influence is more lasting than majority influence, as Moscovici proposed, is not yet clear. It may be that the influence achieved by members of a group derives more from their overall credibility and perceived commitment to the group than from their particular behavioural style or how many allies they have (Turner, 1991). This is nowhere more true than in the case of leaders, which we now consider.

## LEADERSHIP

The capacity of one person to influence others has long been a subject of fascination, both popular and academic. While early researchers sought to identify the individual qualities that led particular persons to emerge as group leaders, subsequent attention has been given to the effectiveness of those who are appointed to a formal leadership role, usually within a large organization. Although the majority of such studies have been undertaken in business organizations, we may anticipate that substantially similar issues do also arise within schools, hospitals, universities, prisons, and government organizations.

The effectiveness of a leader at the very top of a large organization may sometimes be assessed on the basis of the whole organization's success. More usually effectiveness has been assessed by looking at the performance of the team or small group for whom the leader is responsible.

This shift of attention from leadership emergence to leadership effectiveness means that leadership study can no longer be thought of as the study of *all* kinds of social influence exerted by a single individual in a group, but only of those achievable by someone appointed or elected to a leadership role. Other types of influence by a single individual will certainly also occur in groups and these will be addressed in the rest of this chapter.

## Obedience

The legitimacy accorded to someone's right to command others, simply because he or she has been appointed to a leadership role, was vividly illustrated by the work of Milgram (1974). Milgram created a situation in which experimental subjects found that they were being asked to administer what appeared to be increasingly dangerous levels of electric shocks to another person, as part of a programme of psychological research. Around two-thirds of his experimental subjects none the less continued to obey their instructions, right up to a level of shock that would in fact endanger life. These findings from the United States have been repeated in seven other countries (Smith & Bond, 1993), and are often used to illustrate the dangers of dictatorial or unscrupulous leadership. However, both Milgram and those who made similar studies in Germany, The Netherlands, and Australia found that under some circumstances obedience fell almost to zero. This happened when other experimental accomplices in the experimental setting refused to carry out their part in the administration of the shocks. In other words, the obedience demanded of the subjects was obtained only when there were no other dissenting group members present. Just as the studies of group polarization find effects that are much attenuated when a leader is present, so do the obedience studies find effects that are much weakened when other group members are present.

If we are to understand the effects attributable to leadership, we must therefore give most attention to settings in which both leaders and group members are actually present.

## Leadership style

Leadership theorists have frequently attempted to identify particular patterns of leadership behaviour that are associated with successful team performance. In the early part of the twentieth century it was believed that such patterns, or leadership traits, were inborn qualities. The optimism of the 1950s and 1960s suggested instead that one could train leaders to adopt the styles of behaviour that were found to be most effective. A variety of leader styles were identified, many of them influenced by the distinction between an authoritarian or task-centred style and a more democratic or person-centred style.

Extensive research at the University of Michigan, for instance, provided an empirical base for the "human relations" school of management theorizing (Likert, 1961). By conducting surveys in a wide variety of organizations it was found that the supervisors of high-performing teams were perceived as more "employee-oriented", spending more time on planning and training and less on checking up on their teams. The breadth of data collected by the Michigan researchers was impressive, but its principal weakness lay in the fact that it all came from field surveys. As in the case of other types of correlational study, one cannot be sure whether there is a causal link between two variables found to be correlated. Subsequent researchers were able to show in laboratory experiments that by instructing workers who were experimental accomplices to work either slow or fast, it was quite possible to elicit different styles of leadership from their supervisors. So for instance in the Likert findings, the fact that a supervisor checked up less often on a particular team might not be the cause of that team's high performance, but rather a consequence of the fact that the supervisor already knew that this was a high-performing, trustworthy team.

## Contingency theories

A second difficulty with the identification of effective leader styles has been that different research groups came up with differing answers as to which were the most effective styles. Several theorists have attempted to cope with this dilemma by formulating what have become known as contingency theories. These theories attempt to specify which type of leadership environment requires what style of leadership behaviour. The best known of these was Fiedler's (1967) theory, in which he proposed that the situations where leaders operated could be rank ordered in terms of their favourability in permitting the leader to exert influence.

In Fiedler's original model, the most favourable setting was one in which team members liked the leader, the task was a structured one and the leader's position carried the right to exert substantial power. Later, he acknowledged that other factors may also influence the favourability of the leader's situation. In contrast to the Michigan researchers, Fiedler believes that leaders have relatively poor capacity to modify their leadership styles, and that therefore the optimal procedure is to diagnose the leader's style, and ensure their placement in the type of setting where that style is effective (Fiedler & Chemers, 1984). His "LPC" measure of style uses a series of ratings completed by the leader, which evaluate the worst subordinate he or she has ever worked with. As one might expect, a more authoritarian or task-oriented leader tends to rate such a person negatively, whereas a more participative or relationship-oriented leader gives more moderate ratings. However, it appears that high and low LPC leaders' behaviour does in fact vary somewhat, depending on the situation in which they find themselves (Smith & Peterson, 1988). The predictions of Fiedler's theory are shown in Figure 2.

Both the validity of Fiedler's measure of leader style, and the capacity of his model to specify situation favourability have been strongly criticized (Schriesheim & Kerr, 1977). Despite this, the theory continues to attract adherents and Fiedler has progressively improved it by examining the contribution of additional leader qualities such as intelligence and prior experience (Fiedler & Garcia, 1987).

A second contingency theory of leadership is that advanced by Vroom and Yetton (1973). These authors see leaders as able to select the leadership style required for any particular specific decision. Their theory comes in the form of a series of questions a manager may ask as to the attributes of the

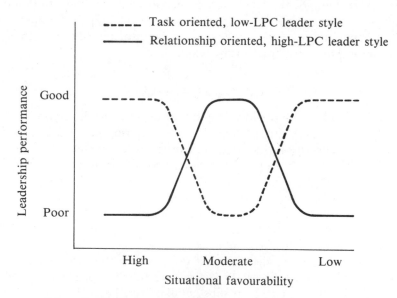

*Figure 2*   Fiedler's predictions as to leadership effectiveness

particular decision to be taken. Depending on answers to seven questions, the model will prescribe an appropriate style, ranging from autocratic decision-making to full team participation. Tests of the model have shown that where managers used the prescribed style, decisions are usually more effective (Vroom & Jago, 1988).

## Rethinking the question: what is leadership?

Contingency theories were mostly formulated some time ago, and have not gained increasing adherence with the passage of time. In order to consider why this might be so, we must reflect on the overall changes occurring within the field of psychology since the early 1970s. From being a predominantly behaviourist enterprise, psychology has increasingly turned to investigating cognitive processes. From this perspective, it is easy to see that many of the conceptions of leadership held by theorists have been implicitly behaviourist. Leadership has been seen as something that a leader does to a subordinate, much in the way that behaviourists thought of stimuli as evoking responses. But thinking about relations between leaders and subordinates in this manner requires a great many simplifications of what happens in practical settings. As was noted earlier, subordinates are well able to influence their leaders. By working faster or slower, they can evoke predictable responses from their superiors. Thus, the leader's relation to the group must be thought of as a two-way rather than a one-way influence process. Attention is therefore required not only to the effects of a precise-sounding "leader style", but also to the manner in which leaders and their subordinates interpret the meaning of one another's actions. In line with this, many studies have explored such issues as how leaders choose between different possible responses to a subordinate who is, for instance, late for work or who does poor work.

A second simplification that leadership theorists have often found necessary can also be linked to the predominant emphases of psychology as a whole. Just as researchers in many fields sought to control extraneous influences by creating precisely defined experimental conditions, so leadership theorists have mostly examined only the links between leaders and their immediate subordinates. In practice, of course, leaders devote substantial amounts of time to their links with their own superiors, relevant colleagues and many others within and sometimes outside the organization in which they work. Long ago, Pelz (1951) showed that leaders' effectiveness as judged by their subordinates was strongly related to how well the leaders got on with their own superiors. Likert (1961) formulated what he termed a "linking pin theory" of leadership, which emphasised the leader's importance in linking the different groups within a large organization. Later theorists have developed this notion and reformulated the concept of leadership to emphasize the manner in which leader effectiveness can be thought of as the successful management of the conflicting needs and demands of the "role set" (Graen

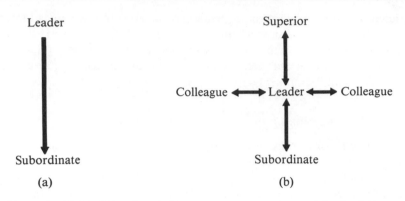

*Figure 3* (a) Traditional and (b) contemporary patterns of leader influence

& Cashman, 1975; Smith & Peterson, 1988). The role set comprises all those people who make demands on the occupant of a particular role. This changing emphasis of leadership study is illustrated in Figure 3.

Such a reformulation provides a much more realistic model of the behaviour of leaders in organizations, but it poses additional problems for researchers. If we acknowledge that the different members of a leader's role set each have valid demands that they wish to make on the leader, how do we evaluate the leader's effectiveness? Since the various demands are likely to be at least partially incompatible, the various possible sources of evaluation are likely to give us different answers. Tsui's (1984) study of Californian managers showed that this problem was not insuperable. There was in fact some consensus among her sample of role set members as to which were the most effective managers.

Even though Tsui found that role set members may to some extent agree as to a leader's effectiveness or ineffectiveness, it is not likely that the leader will be displaying the same leader style toward them all. Once we relinquish the myth that leaders relate only to their subordinates we need to examine a fuller range of ways in which leaders might influence others around them.

## CLASSIFICATION OF SOCIAL INFLUENCE STRATEGIES

French and Raven (1959) proposed that there are basically five ways in which we might influence one another. Later versions have added a sixth (Raven & Rubin, 1983). The classification provides three bases for distinguishing forms of social influence. First, it separates influence that depends on a continuing relationship with the influencing agent from that which does not. Second, it distinguishes influence based on continuing surveillance by the influence agent from that which is not. Finally, it distinguishes influence in the intended direction from that in which the effect is the opposite of that intended. A simplified version of the classification of these types is shown in Figure 4.

If we consider the application of the Raven-Rubin model to influence with a leader's role set, there are clearly some bases for influence that are available to a leader only for influencing subordinates. In particular, coercive power and legitimate power fall into this category. The power to coerce and to reward, and the legitimate right to give orders to subordinates, are inherent in the role definition of many appointed and elected leaders, although the use of these powers cannot necessarily be relied on to maximize leader effectiveness. However, in dealing with organizational colleagues and superiors, leaders must perforce rely mainly on the remaining three bases of influence. The term referent power describes influence based on the other's liking for oneself. Although such influence is no doubt widespread within (and outside of) organizations it is less likely to be openly acknowledged than is influence based on the provision of information and the demonstration of expertise.

The Raven and Rubin typology of social power has proved rather attractive to researchers, who have sought to delineate how widely each of the bases of social influence is employed in different settings. Unfortunately the questionnaire employed in many of these studies has major deficiencies (Podsakoff & Schriesheim, 1985). It yields scores that imply that the more one basis of influence is used, the less are the other bases used. Consequently, these studies do not provide reliable estimates of the frequencies of different types of social influence. However, Kipnis, Schmidt, and Wilkinson (1980) developed an alternative instrument (the "Profile of Organizational Influence Strategies") in which managers are asked to describe their influence strategies and with whom they use which strategy. These researchers distinguish seven types of influence: friendliness, reason, assertiveness, coalitions, higher authority, bargaining, and sanctions. Some of these overlap the Raven-Rubin model, but the inclusion of reason, bargaining, and the forming of coalitions

| Eliciting conditions | Types of power available |
|---|---|
| Continuing social dependence<br>Continuing surveillance | Reward power<br>Coercive power |
| Continuing social dependence<br>No surveillance | Expert power<br>Legitimate power<br>Referent power |
| No continuing social dependence<br>No surveillance | Informational power |

*Figure 4* Raven and Rubin's typology of social influence processes

underlines the range of strategies likely to be used in influencing colleagues and superiors.

The formulation of these typologies thus represents an advance over the earlier excessive reliance on measures of leader style, because they allow for a rather fuller range of possibilities than those embedded in the style measures. It is of course plausible that leaders frequently also influence their subordinates through, for instance, reasoning with them and through the exercise of expertise, rather than through direct reliance on the powers given to them by those who appointed them. If this is so, then it becomes easier to see continuities between the results of traditional studies of leadership, and the rather broader range of studies that have looked at social influence in settings outside of organizations.

## SOCIAL INFLUENCE IN INFORMAL SETTINGS

Christie and Geis (1970) attempted to analyse the techniques used by those who proved influential in informal and unstructured settings. For instance, they assembled groups of three and placed ten dollars on the table. They then stated that any two of the three people present could have the money, once they had agreed how the money would be divided between them. By definition, the third person got nothing. The experimental subjects who prospered under circumstances such as these were those whom Christie and Geis termed Machiavellians. Drawing on the prescriptions of the Renaissance master of intrigue and diplomacy, Machiavelli, they devised a questionnaire, which they named the "Mach" scale. This was intended to distinguish those who would behave in an equally ruthless manner within their experimental setting. As predicted, high Mach scorers did particularly well in gaining a large share of the money on the table. While Christie and Geis were thus successful in identifying Machiavellians, they did rather less well in identifying exactly what it was that they did that contributed to their success. Having examined Machiavellian behaviour in a dozen experiments they conclude that Machiavellian skill lies not so much in what is done as in the timing of Machiavellians' actions. The situations in which Machiavellians were found to do well were those in which people meet face-to-face, improvisation is at a premium, and the situation arouses what Christie and Geis call "irrelevant affect". Presumably the irrelevant affect experienced by low Machiavellians in the ten-dollar game would have to do with the unfairness of the third party getting nothing.

The exercise of Machiavellian skills is certainly not absent from life within many formal organizations, but the circumstances in which it is likely to be most favoured occur in more transient situations. Cialdini (1988) reviews social influence strategies in situations involving the selling of a product. Drawing on the findings of cognitive psychologists concerning the "mindlessness" of many of our everyday actions (Langer, 1978), he shows how salespeople are sometimes able to manipulate customers who are not on their guard. He proposes that influence can occur in any of six ways.

First, a salesperson may rely on the norm of reciprocity. By giving a free sample or a free survey of one's house, a sense of indebtedness is instilled, which the purchaser may feel should be repaid. Second, if the salesperson can obtain a small initial commitment, the purchaser will be more willing to make a greater commitment later. This "foot-in-the-door" effect was demonstrated experimentally by Freedman and Fraser (1966). Third, "social proof" may be drawn on, to establish that a product or service is good. This would be done through inviting conformity with the habits of others whom one might wish to emulate.

The fourth and fifth strategies rest on the findings established by leadership researchers and others that people accept influence from those whom they like and whom they see as authoritative. Salespeople therefore seek to establish their attractiveness, expertise, and similarity to the purchaser. Researchers into the process of ingratiation have identified some of the ways in which this may be done (Jones, 1964). For instance, ingratiators may compliment their target persons, emphasize the similarity of their views, and conceal their intentions to be influential. Pandey (1986) found that the ingratiation tactics favoured in India differed somewhat from Jones's US results. Name dropping and denigrating oneself were among the strategies favoured. Studies of the ways in which US managers exert upward influence over their own bosses also suggest that where reasoned argument fails many of these tactics of ingratiation will be employed (Porter, Allen, & Angle, 1981).

Finally, Cialdini (1988) points out that we frequently respond positively to the information that a product is scarce, forbidden, or about to be withdrawn.

Cialdini's list of types of influence strategy may be compared with those obtained by Kipnis et al. (1980) within organizations. There is clearly substantial overlap, but there are differences also. These may stem from the more transient relationship that some types of salesperson are likely to have with their customers. To the extent that a salesperson is concerned about maintaining the long-term satisfaction of customers, the range of available influence strategies will become increasingly similar to those found in organizations. Where a quick sale is all that counts, we may expect greatest use of Machiavellian strategies, such as those based on the creation of spurious indebtedness, the foot-in-the-door, and the exaggeration of scarcity.

Whatever effectiveness such sales techniques have rests on the fact that a sale is concluded on the spot. Where influence effectiveness is measured by its effect on longer-term behaviour, rates of compliance are likely to be very much weaker. Even in situations where an influence agent has substantial authority and expertise, they may not be very influential. For instance Ley (1982) has shown that less than half of the instructions given by doctors to take medicines or to modify behaviour in particular ways are subsequently carried out by the patients who consulted them.

## CHARISMA

Our exploration of the diversity of influence strategies has left to one side a contrasting development in the study of leadership. The nineteenth-century sociologist Max Weber saw charisma as one possible basis for the influential powers of leaders. He saw charisma as an almost magical or religiously endowed quality through which certain leaders communicated a vision of the future or of the good life to their followers.

Some theorists of leadership have given new life to this concept (Bryman, 1992; Conger & Kanungo, 1988). Contrary to role-set theorists, who might seem to be arguing that all influence in organizations is to be thought of as leadership, these authors rely on the argument that leadership must be distinguished from management. Management is seen as routine administration, while the term leadership is reserved for those acts of influence that seek to create change and innovation. Such acts are more likely to be found at the very top of large organizations, or governments. It is suggested that effective leadership in this sense requires the types of charismatic skills that Weber had in mind. Case studies of some of the most charismatic business leaders are widely available (Bryman, 1992).

A somewhat different approach has been taken by Bass (1985), who has developed a questionnaire measure of perceived charismatic leader style. Bass sees charisma as having potential importance for leaders at all levels in organisations, not just at the top. However, all the current theorists of charisma would agree that the crucial distinction between their approach and earlier studies of leader style is that charismatic leaders establish an intense emotional bond with their followers that rests on a mutually shared vision. This contrasts with the earlier conception of leader style as a means of one-way downward influence, but it leaves relatively unexamined the manner in which the two-way bond is established.

## SOCIAL INFLUENCE AS NEGOTIATION

The approaches to influence discussed earlier in this chapter imply that whether we are considering charisma, the way in which managers respond to their role set, or the activities of salespeople, it may be useful to think of all types of social influence as types of negotiation. Use of the word "negotiation" immediately implies that the process being considered is a two-way process. The type of negotiation implicit in influence need not entail overt bargaining, but will involve each party responding to the prior behaviours of the other. Hosking and Morley (1992) present an analysis of this kind, focused on the "social psychology of organizing". For them, the essence of social influence is the negotiation of what they call "order", by which term they mean a shared interpretation of events. Within this perspective, the manner in which all of the types of social influence surveyed in this chapter achieve their effect is by one or both parties changing the meaning they give to an event or an action. This can include the decision of an experimental subject as to the length of a line, the decision of a purchaser that something is worth buying, and the agreement between organization members as to how to handle a particular event. The virtue of this approach is that it offers to unify what has become a diverse field of inquiry, but it can do so only conceptually. If we wish to specify whether some participants in the negotiation of order are likely to be more powerful than others, then we must return to the issues addressed throughout this chapter. In their differing ways, each group of researchers has made proposals as to what it is that makes some of us more powerful or persuasive than others.

## FURTHER READING

Bryman, A. (1992). *Charisma and leadership in organizations*. London: Sage.

Cialdini, R. B. (1988). *Influence: Science and practice*. Glenview, IL: Scott, Foresman.

Fiedler, F. E., & Garcia, J. E. (1987). *New approaches to effective leadership: Cognitive resources and organizational performance*. New York: Wiley.

Smith, P. B., & Peterson, M. F. (1988). *Leadership, organizations and culture*. London: Sage.

Turner, J. C. (1991). *Social influence*. Milton Keynes: Open University Press.

## REFERENCES

Abrams, D., Wetherell, M., Cochrane, S., Hogg, M., & Turner, J. C. (1990). Knowing what to think by knowing who you are: Self-categorisation and the nature of norm formation, conformity and group polarisation. *British Journal of Social Psychology*, *29*, 97–119.

Allen, V., & Levine, J. M (1968). Social support, dissent and conformity. *Sociometry*, *31*, 138–149.

Asch, S. (1951). Effects of group pressure upon the modification and distortion of judgments. In H. Guetzkow (Ed.) *Groups, leadership and men* (pp. 177–190). Pittsburgh, PA: Carnegie.

Bass, B. M. (1985). *Leadership and performance beyond expectations*. New York: Free Press.

Brickner, M. A., Ostrom, T. M., & Harkins, S. G. (1986). Effects of personal involvement: Thought-provoking implications for social loafing. *Journal of Personality and Social Psychology*, *51*, 763–769.

Brown, R. (1986). *Social psychology: The second edition*. New York: Free Press.

Bryman, A. (1992). *Charisma and leadership in organizations*. London: Sage.

Christie, R., & Geis, F. (1970). *Studies in Machiavellianism*. New York: Academic Press.

Cialdini, R. B. (1988). *Influence: Science and practice*. Glenview, IL: Scott, Foresman.

Clark, R. D., & Maass, A. (1988). The role of social categorisation and perceived source credibility in minority influence. *European Journal of Social Psychology*, *18*, 381–394.

Conger, J. A., & Kanungo, R. N. (Eds) (1988). *Charismatic leadership: The elusive factor in organizational effectiveness*. San Francisco, CA: Jossey-Bass.

Deutsch, M., & Gerard, H. B. (1955). A study of normative and informational social influence. *Journal of Abnormal and Social Psychology*, *51*, 629–636.

Doise, W. (1969). Intergroup relations and polarization of individual and collective judgments. *Journal of Personality and Social Psychology*, *12*, 136–143.

Fiedler, F. E. (1967). *A theory of leadership effectiveness*. New York: McGraw-Hill.

Fiedler, F. E., & Chemers, M. (1984). *Improving leadership effectiveness: The leader match concept*. New York: Wiley.

Fiedler, F. E., & Garcia, J. E. (1987). *New approaches to effective leadership: Cognitive resources and organizational performance*. New York: Wiley.

Freedman, J. L., & Fraser, S. C. (1966). Compliance without pressure: The foot-in-the-door technique. *Journal of Personality and Social Psychology*, *4*, 195–202.

French, J. R. P., & Raven, B. H. (1959). The bases of social power. In D. Cartwright (Ed.) *Studies in social power* (pp. 150–167). Ann Arbor, MI: Institute for Social Research, University of Michigan.

Friend, R., Rafferty, Y., & Bramel, D. (1990). A puzzling misinterpretation of the Asch "conformity" study. *European Journal of Social Psychology*, *20*, 29–44.

Graen, G. B., & Cashman, J. F. (1975). A role-making model of leadership in formal organizations. In J. G. Hunt & L. L. Larson (Eds) *Leadership frontiers* (pp. 143–165). Kent, OH: Kent State University Press.

Hosking, D. M., & Morley, I. (1992). *The social psychology of organising*. London: Sage.

Jesuino, J. (1986). Influence of leadership processes on group polarisation. *European Journal of Social Psychology*, *16*, 413–424.

Jones, E. E. (1964). *Ingratiation: A social psychological analysis*. New York: Appleton-Century-Crofts.

Kipnis, D., Schmidt, S. M., & Wilkinson, I. (1980). Intraorganizational influence tactics: Explorations in getting one's way. *Journal of Applied Psychology*, *65*, 440–452.

Kravitz, D. A., & Martin B. (1986). Ringelmann rediscovered: The original article. *Journal of Personality and Social Psychology*, *50*, 936–941.

Langer, E. (1978). Rethinking the role of thought in social interaction. In J. H. Harvey, W. J. Ickes, & R. F. Kidd (Eds) *New directions in attribution research* (vol. 2, pp. 35–58). New York: Halstead.

Latané, B., Williams, K., & Harkins, S. G. (1979). Many hands make light work: The causes and consequences of social loafing. *Journal of Personality and Social Psychology*, *37*, 822–832.

Ley, P. (1982). Satisfaction, compliance and communication. *British Journal of Clinical Psychology*, *21*, 241–254.

Likert, R. (1961). *New patterns of management*. New York: McGraw-Hill.

Milgram, S. (1974). *Obedience to authority*. New York: Harper & Row.

Moscovici, S. (1976). *Social influence and social change*. London: Academic Press.

Moscovici, S. (1980). Towards a theory of conversion behavior. In L. Berkowitz (Ed.) *Advances in experimental social psychology*, *13*, 209–239.

Nemeth, C., Swedlund, M., & Kanki, B. (1974). Patterning of the minority's responses and their influence on the majority. *European Journal of Social Psychology*, *4*, 53–64.

Pandey, J. (1986). Sociocultural perspectives on ingratiation. In B. A. Maher & W. B. Maher (Eds) *Progress in experimental personality research*, *14*, 205–229.

Pelz, D. C. (1951). Leadership within a hierarchical organisation. *Journal of Social Issues*, *7*, 49–55.

Podsakoff, P. M., & Schriesheim, C. A. (1985). Field studies of French and Raven's bases of social power: Critique, reanalysis and suggestions for future research. *Psychological Bulletin*, *97*, 387–411.

Porter, L. W., Allen, R. W., & Angle, H. L. (1981). The politics of upward influence in organizations. In L. L. Cummings & B. M. Staw (Eds) *Research in Organizational Behavior*, *3*, 109–149.

Raven, B. H., & Rubin, J. Z. (1983). *Social psychology*. New York: Wiley.

Schriesheim, C. A., & Kerr, S. (1977). Theories and measures of leadership: A critical appraisal of current and future directions. In J. G. Hunt & L. L. Larson (Eds) *Leadership: The cutting edge* (pp. 9–45). Carbondale, IL: Southern Illinois University Press.

Semin, G., & Glendon, A. (1973). Polarisation and the established group. *British Journal of Social and Clinical Psychology*, *12*, 113–121.

Smith, P. B., & Bond, M. H. (1993). *Social psychology across cultures: Analysis and perspectives*. Hemel Hempstead: Harvester-Wheatsheaf.

Smith, P. B., & Peterson, M. F. (1988). *Leadership, organizations and culture*. London: Sage.

Stoner, J. A. F. (1961). *A comparison of individual and group decisions involving risk*. Unpublished master's thesis, Massachusetts Institute of Technology.

Tsui, A. S. (1984). A role set analysis of managerial reputation. *Organizational Behavior and Human Performance*, *34*, 64–96.

Turner, J. C. (1991). *Social influence*. Milton Keynes: Open University Press.

Vroom, V. H., & Jago, A. (1988). *The new leadership: Managing participation in organizations*. Englewood Cliffs, NJ: Prentice-Hall.

Vroom, V. H., & Yetton, P. W. (1973). *Leadership and decision-making*. Pittsburgh, PA: University of Pittsburgh Press.

Zajonc, R. B. (1965). Social facilitation. *Science*, *149*, 269–274.

# 3

# ATTRIBUTION AND SOCIAL COGNITION

## David J. Schneider
### Rice University, Texas, USA

Social cognition may be defined as the study of how people understand their social worlds. It is, in short, the cognition of people, their behaviour, and the settings in which that behaviour occurs. This definition is broad enough to encompass all social cognition research and theory, but it is also vague. What exactly does social cognition cover?

It first concerns the perception of people, what has traditionally been called person perception (Schneider, Hastorf, & Ellsworth, 1979). There are three classic person perception problems. First, how do we interpret and describe the behaviour of self and others (attribution); more specifically, what do we infer about people from behaviour and whatever other information we may have? Second, how do we integrate that information into a coherent whole. Third, are our perceptions and inferences about others accurate?

The field of person perception has deep roots in social psychology; there has been speculation about our perceptions of self and others as long as there has been social analysis. Person perception reached its high flowering during the period from 1950 to 1980, and it was especially nourished by developments surrounding attribution theory, to be discussed shortly. Since the 1980s, however, the traditional areas of person perception have more or less been supplanted by what is called social cognition. Social cognition differs from the older field of person perception less in terms of phenomena under investigation as in the approach (see Fiske & Taylor, 1991; Ostrom, 1984; Schneider, 1991 for contrasting views).

Traditional person perception tended to take its lead from the larger area of social psychology which was concerned with the content of our thoughts about others on the reasonable assumption that this would help predict our behaviours toward them. Early studies dealt with the accuracy of our inferences about others, with factors affecting the evaluative nature of impressions, with how impressions were organized, with whether causes of behaviour were internal or external. That is not to say that process considerations were ignored, but only that they tended to be the tail wagged by the dog of emphasis on what people thought.

Social cognition, on the other hand, reverses this relative emphasis by focusing more heavily on how information is processed. Whereas inferences of evaluative traits or specific attributions used to be the dependent measures of choice, in the present day memory, reaction time, and other microscopically oriented process measures are favoured. That is in part because social cognition tends to ally itself with the larger field of cognitive psychology to such an extent that it is often quite impossible to know where one begins and the other leaves off. In this chapter we first discuss classic perception issues, and then we shall summarize some of the approaches taken by social cognition research.

# ACCURACY

## EMOTIONS

Whether people can be and are accurate in their perceptions of others is an obvious problem, and it was the first intensively studied issue in the person perception area. Early studies on accuracy of perception of emotional expression were stimulated by Darwin's speculations that emotional expression is evolutionarily determined and hence "hard-wired"; thus emotional expression should be cross-culturally invariant and presumably easily recognized. Early studies in this area (see Schneider et al., 1979) often found that people could not even agree on the precise labels to attach to emotional expression's let alone judge them accurately, but more careful contemporary work (Ekman & Friesen, 1975) has generally found a high degree of both agreement among perceivers and accuracy for six basic emotions (sadness, happiness, anger, fear, disgust, and surprise) judged from standard stimuli. That is not to suggest that every person conveys anger in exactly the same way or that all ways of expressing anger are easily recognized. Also some less central emotions such as wonderment or bewilderment or blends of emotions such as the horror and curiosity that might accompany seeing a grisly accident, may not be easily recognized. However, there are standard expressions of standard emotions, and these are easily recognized, as common sense would suggest.

## TRAITS

Early studies of accuracy of perceptions of personality were also not particularly promising (Taft, 1955). In addition, it is now widely recognized that two major methodological problems plague this area. The first identified by Cronbach (1955) deals with the measurement of accuracy. Cronbach showed that when we measure accuracy as a departure of perceivers' judgements from a criterion (say, ratings of target's introversion), the differences may be due to many factors. For example, some perceivers may be inaccurate because they see everyone as being too introverted although they correctly see that Joseph is more introverted than Doris, who is in turn more introverted than Terry. Another perceiver might be quite accurate in the sense that she correctly sees that people are, on average, moderately introverted but cannot do a good job of discriminating how introverted individual targets are. Who is the more accurate? Simply calculating accuracy as a discrepancy of prediction from criterion might make the second perceiver more accurate, simply because her judgements are more in the "right ballpark", even though she doesn't have a clue as to which of several people is the more introverted. This does not seem quite right. Thus, there are many land-mines in the measurement of accuracy.

A second problem has come to be called the criterion problem (Schneider et al., 1979). How do we know how much hostility, self-esteem, extraversion, and so on people really have, especially when expression of these traits is likely to vary considerably over situations and encounters with individual perceivers? Not only do we not have objective, perfectly clear measures of traits such as introversion, but also most of us vary in how introverted we are from situation to situation.

For these and other reasons accuracy research declined during the 1960s and 1970s. However, during the 1980s, the area got a new lease on life. Swann (1984), Funder (1987), and others argued that people can be accurate if given a clear criterion (often behavioural) and rich information about the people they are judging. One interesting line of research shows that people tend to be more accurate for traits that are highly visible (e.g., extraversion) than for those which are less immediately visible (e.g., emotional stability) (Park & Judd, 1989; Watson, 1989).

# ATTRIBUTION

## THE CLASSIC HEIDER MODEL

Attribution theory deals with how we attribute traits, motives, and abilities to people from observations of their behaviour. Since the late 1960s, attribution models have been investigated extensively within social psychology and have been applied to problems not only in social psychology but also in clinical, personality, and developmental psychology.

Attribution theory was first proposed by Fritz Heider (1958). However, his version of the theory was not especially amenable to experimental test; it is unlikely that the theory would have become a dominating force in modern social cognition and social psychology more generally without "translations" by Jones & Davis (1965) and Kelley (1967). Heider's original formulation focused on how we attribute the causes of behaviour. In an analogy with the world of physical causality, he noted that objects behave the ways they do because of the joint influence of their own qualities that *dispose* them to behave in certain ways (dispositional qualities) and environmental forces. For example, the roundness of balls disposes them to roll when pushed, and the mass of large buildings does not dispose them to roll when force is applied. On the other hand, rubber balls may simply compress or disintegrate when a huge force is applied, whereas a tall building would sway. Heider argued that people are also disposed to behave in particular ways when various kinds of forces are applied to them. The dispositional properties of some people make them violent in the face of frustration while others would just cry. But even people who are dispositionally violent do not always hit and abuse; there must be a precipitating external force.

These two kinds of forces, sometimes called internal and external (mirroring an earlier distinction by Heider's friend, Kurt Lewin, between own and induced forces), must both be present for behaviour to occur. However, in a given situation, a perceiver may see behaviour as caused relatively more by one force or another. The behaviour of a violent criminal is likely to be seen as caused by dispositional forces ("He is a violent person"), whereas the ritualized behaviour of a groom at his wedding is more likely to be seen as caused by strong situational forces. So long as we remember that both kinds of forces are necessary for behaviour, it makes a certain amount of sense to see some behaviours as internally or dispositionally caused and others as having been influenced more by the situation. Roughly this corresponds to the common distinction between "She did it because she wanted to" vs "She did it because she had to".

The internal—external cause distinction is important because it allows us to predict and sometimes control the behaviour of others. If I know you are generally kind, I can predict that you will respond to my request for a loan favourably. However, if I know that you are kind only when you are in a good mood or when you are approached with a particularly strong external request, I may try to work on these external factors before hitting you up.

## KELLEY'S MODEL

### Types of information

The essential question of attribution theory is how we make those discriminations. Harold Kelley's (1967) theory has been the most influential guide. He argued that people look at three forms of information. Given that a person has performed a discrete behaviour or had a particular reaction (which is Kelley's starting-point), *consensus information* refers to how many other people performed the same behaviour. In other words, how unusual is the behaviour? If Janice orders fish at the restaurant (the *behaviour*), and most other people do the same, we would say that the consensus information for that behaviour is high. Conversely if she orders fish and is the only person to do so, consensus is low. Second, we might ask how consistent her behaviour is. Does she always order seafood in this restaurant? If so, the behaviour is consistent (high *consistency*), and if not her behaviour is inconsistent with past behaviour. Finally, we might ask about Janice's behaviour in other situations. Does she always order seafood, even when not in a seafood restaurant? Does she often buy fish at the local market. If her ordering seafood is restricted to this particular restaurant, her behaviour is distinctive (high *distinctiveness*), but if she shows a behavioural fondness for seafood in many situations, the distinctiveness of her present behaviour is low.

When one combines these three kinds of information, there are eight possible combinations. However, only two are directly relevant to the distinction between internal and external causality. According to Kelley internal, dispositional attributions (what he calls actor attributions) ought to be particularly high with a pattern of low consensus (Janice is the only person who orders fish), low distinctiveness (she almost always orders seafood wherever she is), and high consistency (she almost always orders fish at this restaurant). Janice must really love fish, and consequently she is disposed to order it. Conversely with high consensus (everyone orders fish), high distinctiveness (Janice almost never orders fish elsewhere), and high consistency (she always orders fish here), we would tend to think that Janice's behaviour is controlled mostly externally, by the situation − the fish is good.

## Criticisms

This model has generated hundreds of empirical studies that confirm it in broad outline, but we might argue that it is unnecessarily complex. It requires that people have access to three different kinds of information and think in terms of patterns of information. Surely that is a bit too much to ask of people who, after all, must form their attributions on the fly and often without much reflection. A group of psychologists influenced by Jaspars (1983) has suggested that people really respond more simply.

The most fully worked out such model is that of Hilton and Slugoski (1986). They argue that each type of information is coordinated with a particular kind of attribution. For example, consensus information affects primarily internal attributions, distinctiveness information plays a major role in situation attributions, and consistency affects attributions to circumstance. People then make attributions to the information that seems to stand out, to be abnormal in the context. So if Janice is the only person to order fish, she stands out and the attribution will be to her dispositions. Conversely, if she orders fish only at this restaurant and never eats it elsewhere, the attribution would be to the restaurant and its way of fixing fish. The *abnormal conditions model* has the virtue of being simple, and it generally predicts attributions at least as well, and often better, than the more complex Kelley model.

Many other factors beyond those identified by Kelley affect the attribution process. For example, some traits and behaviours, typically those that are active, tend to be seen as dispositionally caused whereas emotional reactions tend to be seen as more often caused by external stimuli (Fiedler & Semin, 1988; Van Kleeck, Hillger, & Brown, 1988). Also the kinds of attributions that we make are highly sensitive to conversational norms and to what we assume other people know (McGill, 1989; Turnbull & Slugoski, 1988); "Why did John shout?" will be answered differently depending on whether these contextual factors focus attention on why John shouted as opposed to Jim, or why John shouted instead of leaving the situation.

43

## ATTRIBUTIONAL BIAS

One problem with traditional attribution models has been that perceivers do not always follow them closely. It is not merely that predictions from the models do not always "come out"; if that were the case we might simply say that the models were wrong. Rather, the violations of the models tend to be systematic and biased. One kind of bias has been called egocentric; sometimes we attribute our behaviour and the behaviour of others in self-serving ways. For example, I may decide that poor student performance on my exams is due to their laziness or stupidity rather than to my poor teaching.

Such bias does occur (Hewstone, 1989), but the bias that has received the most research attention has been the tendency to downplay information about the situational causes of behaviour; this leads us to see the behaviour of others as less determined by situational forces that it should be, whereas own behaviour is more often seen as situationally determined (Jones & Nisbett, 1972). In general we assign too much dispositional impact to the behaviour of others, a feature that has come to be known as the fundamental attribution error.

Perhaps the most provocative explanation of this comes from Daniel Gilbert. Following research of Uleman and his students (Newman & Uleman, 1989) and of Trope (1986), Gilbert (1989) argues that perceivers first identify a bit of behaviour ("a kind act"), and then more or less automatically assume a dispositional explanation ("It was committed by a kind person"). Subsequently the perceiver may correct this dispositional inference by recognizing that everyone else in the situation also behaved kindly or that more generally there were strong situational forces encouraging kind behaviour. However, this correction requires some thought and can easily be disrupted by other demands on the person's thought processes. So in practice we often fail to perform the correction stage properly, and as a result we tend to see people as stronger authors of their behaviour than we ought.

# INFORMATION INTEGRATION

After determining what other people are like, perceivers must integrate that diverse information about them. Sometimes this information is extended in time as when we observe the target's behaviour over a lengthy period. Sometimes the information is simultaneously presented as when we take into account information about what a person is saying as well as how she is saying it, her facial expressions, and the like.

# THE WEIGHTED AVERAGING MODEL

## Information weighting and averaging

While various models for how this information is integrated have been proposed, the most popular was proposed by Norman Anderson (1981), who argues that judgements are weighted averages of incoming information. So just as a final grade in a course is some average of all the exam, paper, and other grades accumulated throughout the course, so judgements about people's traits, likeability, job suitability, and so on, are assumed to be averages of relevant behaviours and other information. If I am trying to determine whether Jon will make a good research assistant, I may take into account his grades in classes, his demeanour, my observations of whether he shows up for appointments on time, even how he dresses.

Further, just as in a course some grades count more than others, so in life some kinds of information are seen as more diagnostic or important. In deciding about Jon, I might, for example, give more weight to behavioural information about his conscientiousness than to his dress or whether he wears glasses. Perceivers weight some information more than other because of perceived diagnosticity; negative information generally receives a higher weight than positive (Skowronski & Carlston, 1989) in part because it may be seen as more diagnostic. Also, information that captures attention more readily, such as unusual behaviour, may be weighted more heavily.

## Primacy effects

One way in which this is important is in explaining primacy effects in impression formation. Research tends to confirm common wisdom that the first information we get about others is more important than the later. One reason for this is that the earlier information is weighted more heavily because it is assumed to be more important or because the perceiver pays less attention to later information because of boredom.

# IMPLICIT PERSONALITY THEORY

Anderson's information integration model deals with how information is combined to reach a final decision, but people also have a sense of how information is interrelated. For example, most people assume that kind people are also warm, a not unreasonable assumption given that the two terms share a good deal of psychological and linguistic similarity. But why do people assume that intelligent people are happy or honest? Psychologically, intelligence and happiness seem to occupy different worlds. The fact that people have assumptions about what traits and other characteristics go with others has come to be known as implicit personality theory (Schneider, 1973). One reason people assume that intelligent people are happy is that in their experiences most of the intelligent people they have known are happy; it may even be that this is generally true. On the other hand, perceptions that these two traits go together may have more to do with our desires to see positive characteristics as going with other positive characteristics, a bias that has long been known as the halo effect (Nisbett & Wilson, 1977a).

# INFORMATION PROCESSING

Since the late 1970s social cognition has been dominated by models, measures, and approaches largely imported from cognitive psychology. That is not to say that traffic between the two areas has been entirely one-sided. Social cognitive researchers have their insights which challenge revealed wisdom from the more basic cognitive psychology.

## BASIC ASSUMPTIONS

### Process is general

Several basic assumptions tend to guide research in social cognition. The first is that cognitive process is general across types of stimuli. While people and physical stimuli such as cars may have different features that attract attention, once one pays attention to one car as opposed to another, or this person rather than that, the consequences for further processing are likely to be the same. Similarly the same rules that govern how we encode, store, and recall information about cars should be the same rules that govern memory for people.

### Schemata and knowledge structures

Knowledge structures are important in guiding our cognitive activities. Classically these knowledge structures were called schemata (singular schema) after the pioneering work of Bartlett (1932), but more recently they have also been called knowledge structures, frames, and stereotypes, among other terms. The basic idea is that our experience tends to be codified, made sensible, and stored in an organized fashion. Our knowledge base about people or most everything else does not merely consist of scraps of information filed away and accessible as dictionary entries. Rather it is more like a well-organized encyclopedia with headings for major topics and many cross-references among topics. I have a well-developed schema for college professor which suggests how people get to be professors, how they spend their days, and even what sorts of traits and other characteristics they are likely to have. I have theories that interrelate all these various kinds of

46

information; for example, I understand that people who are highly extraverted are not likely to want to spend vast hours in musty libraries or smelly labs. I have many cross-references from my professor schema to my schemata of student, university, education in general and the like.

Such schemata affect how we process information. Schemata are rather imperialistic and bossy; our cognitive systems are built to give some priority to what we already know. Pragmatically, we would not want it otherwise. Most social situations represent too complex a stimulus array for us to have the energy or desire to process every single stimulus in its full glory.

## Bias

### The costs of efficiency

This deficiency, however, comes at a price: we are biased in what we experience and remember. Because we can never process all the information we encounter and because our schemata guide our processing, our knowledge is incomplete, biased, and sometimes dead wrong. Social cognition like cognitive psychology generally places a premium on showing that our cognitions are inherently biased. There have been three major traditions that have stimulated this research on cognitive bias in social cognition. First, as we have seen, attribution research has suggested that people do not follow what might be described as rational rules for the processing of behavioural information. Second, memory research during the 1970s and early 1980s documented a large number of memory errors produced by our tendencies to make incoming information consistent with our schemata. Much modern cognitive theory has assumed that the mind is a highly resource-limited "computer", one that needs to compress and abstract incoming information into schemata in the interests of preserving precious memory. Third, the provocative work of Tversky & Kahneman (1974) suggested that in an informationally rich world people must adopt simplified strategies (heuristics) for processing information, and these strategies, while often quite satisfactory and accurate, may in special circumstances produce biases and inaccuracies that cognizers may not fully appreciate.

### Cognitive heuristics

There are many biases introduced by heuristic thinking, but I will list only a couple. One is our tendencies to judge present people or events on the basis of how well they fit known examples from the past. Normally this is a perfectly useful strategy − after all, we do want to benefit from past experience − but sometimes we use bad examples. So, we sometimes ascribe personality features to a person based on his or her physical resemblance to someone else (Lewicki, 1986) or judge whether to admit someone to a graduate programme

47

on the basis of whether he went to the same college as a recent successful or unsuccessful person in the present programme.

We sometimes judge how likely something is by how easy it is to retrieve relevant examples; this is called the availability heuristic. People see the risk of dying from accidents, cancer, and natural disasters as more likely than it actually is, in part because there is usually considerable publicity for such events and so it is easy to remember cases of people who die in these ways. On the other hand, we underestimate the prevalence of other less publicized risks such as emphysema and smallpox vaccination (Slovic, Fischhoff, & Lichtenstein, 1982). In short,we see as more likely those things for which we can find ready examples in memory, but underestimate those that are less salient in memory.

## Automaticity

Some cognitive processes we have discussed may have seemed quite familiar: "Yes, I do that all the time". But with other processes you may have no relevant conscious experiences. In an important paper, Nisbett and Wilson (1977b) argued that we are generally not aware of how we think, of our cognitive processes, as opposed to what we think, the products of these processes. In this most general claim they are surely wrong. I am certainly aware of how I try to solve a complex chess problem, as I try out various moves and keep the results in my head for comparison. However, Nisbett and Wilson were correct in the more limited claim that we *often* do not know how we think. What goes through your head when you answer the question: "What is 2 + 2?" We can only hope nothing.

It is now widely recognized that many of our cognitive processes are so well practised that they become more or less automatic. This term has been used extensively, but it means different things to different psychologists. Generally, when we talk about automatic processes, we mean those that occur largely outside awareness, require few cognitive resources, and are hard if not impossible to control (Bargh, 1989). If I ask you your name, you will generally not be aware of how you retrieved it, you will answer quickly and without much effort, and while you might be able to inhibit actually saying your name aloud in answer to the question, there is probably nothing you could do short of destructive brain surgery to keep your name from popping into your mind.

Whether our cognitive processes are automatic or more controlled is important in everyday life. Suppose I am interviewing a physically handicapped person for a job. Can I ignore the fact that she is in a wheelchair? Probably not; I shall probably think of her as handicapped whether or not I want to do so. Now suppose I think that most handicapped people are hardworking. When I categorize this person as handicapped do I also more or less automatically see her as diligent? Devine (1989) has argued that stereotyping

48

in this way is fairly automatic, but that we can correct our initial, automatic judgements with more controlled thought processes. So I might say to myself that while most handicapped people work hard, this one seems to be on the lazy side. Unfortunately, we sometimes fail to make corrections based on behavioural data we have.

## STAGES

Our processing of social and other information takes places in stages. Typically, one might think of attention, labelling and recognition, memory (itself composed of several well-defined stages), and inferential thinking as major stages.

### Attention

Imagine that I have entered a crowed room, say a cocktail party. My attention will be guided in several ways. I shall probably look at the people rather than at the ceiling light fixtures or the carpeting. And as my gaze sweeps the room, it will pause on some people but not others. That handsome blond man in the Italian suit captures my attention, and so does the distinguished looking woman who seems to have an adoring crowd around her. I see an old friend across the room, and study him for a few seconds – he has put on weight, his hair is greyer, and for a moment I'm not sure that it is my friend. As I make my survey I focus not only on a relatively few people but also on individual features of the people at whom I look. As we all know, attention is highly labile and subject to many influences. If I am looking for a person serving drinks, I scan the room in a different way than if I am trying to find a particular friend.

### Labelling and categorization

At the same time that my attention is landing here and there around the room, other processes are also going on. For one thing, I am implicitly (and sometimes explicitly) labelling and recognizing the things that I see. I know the difference between a man's suit and a dress, between grey and blonde hair. Sometimes that labelling and recognition is quite explicit (the woman with the adoring entourage seems to be powerful; I really should find out who she is), but more often than not it is simply implicit and done without conscious thought. I may also be actively seeking certain sorts of information which further guides attention and labelling. Is that man over there the chap I went to graduate school with 30 years ago? What should I look at to decide?

49

## Category hierarchies

Before we can deal with any stimulus we must label it or place it into one of thousands of cognitive categories we keep available for just such purposes. Everything we encounter can be labelled and categorized in several ways. This thing before me is a computer screen, a part of my computer, an obstruction to my view out the window, a source of eyestrain, and so on. What is this thing? I am a male, a husband, a father, a professor, a psychology professor, a home-owner, grey-haired (very prematurely to be sure), an occasional squash player. Who am I?

One important question stimulated by the influential research of Eleanor Rosch (1978) concerns levels of categorization. The object before me could be described abstractly or relatively concretely as an object, a piece of equipment, a part of a computer, a monitor, an NEC monitor, an NEC 5FG, or an NEC 5FG with serial #XXX. Rosch has argued that there is a basic level of categorization, a level that maximizes the amount of information about uniqueness while giving us some general information. In the example just given "monitor" is probably the basic category. To say it is an object or a part of a computer does not really allow us to distinguish it usefully from the things I would want to see it as different from, but to say it is NEC #XXX is to be entirely too specific. A good but not infallible test of basic categories is what people would call the object without much thinking about it. I suspect that most people would call this piece of equipment a monitor. This might, of course, change. One would imagine that someone working in the NEC warehouse, might point and say "Please get me the 5FG" or (surrounded by similar models) the #XXX. "Get the monitor" would not, in this situation, communicate much.

Whether people, as stimuli, fall so neatly into this kind of framework is an open question. To be sure, the person before me is an animal, a mammal, a human, a male, but then things start to get a bit sticky. Do I proceed: young male, male who is 25, male who was born in July 1967? Or do I proceed: stockbroker, rising star, rising star with a Stanford MBA, rising star with a Stanford MBA working in bonds? This illustrates the simple fact that people are probably subject to quite a few alternative categorizations. Again: a lot depends on relevant contexts. Saying the young man is a father would not tell us much at a meeting of the local Parents' Organization for Better Teaching, but might among a group of other young males who do not have parental responsibilities.

## Category use

Leaving aside the issue of how broad the categories are that we use, another important question is how we pick certain categories. Why do I see the Japanese businessman as Japanese rather than as a businessman? Why do I think of him as male but not necessarily in terms of his golfing prowess? As Brewer (1988) has argued, gender, age, and race are probably basic categories that we use for all people. It would seem strange indeed if after even a brief conversation with someone I could remember her eye colour but not whether she was male or female, old or young, Asian or Caucasian. Beyond that, many categories are given by our cultures. People from most western countries would tend to categorize people in terms of their marital or parental status, but we ordinarily pay little attention to whether an adult has living parents.

Obviously our own motives and goals can also play a role. When I interview people to be my research assistant, their race is much less important than whether they are good students. Our choice of categories is often influenced by which ones we habitually use or have used in the recent past (Smith, 1990). Categories that are "primed" are used more readily and more quickly. The dentist at a party may not be able to help herself from thinking about people in terms of their dental appearance. Physical fitness types may be more inclined to think of others in terms of their physique than I do, and I certainly am prone to categorize people quickly and often in terms of intelligence.

### Exemplars and prototypes

We have been discussing alternative ways of categorizing basically familiar stimuli. But how do we classify things and people we have never seen before? As I walk across an unfamiliar university campus how do I know which people are students, which professors, and which visitors like myself? Advocates of the prototype view suggest that we have abstract representations of categories. When you think of some category, say college professor, you imagine the average professor, the prototypic one, and this prototype embodies the features common to most professors. You decide this new person you have met must be a professor if he or she matches that prototype.

Advocates of the exemplar view argue that we store many examples of each category, and we may even make some implicit decisions as to which are good or poor exemplars. So when you try to judge whether this man before you is a professor or a groundskeeper, you will quickly (and perhaps nonconsciously) think about as many professors and groundskeepers as you can and see whether this unknown person best fits with the exemplars from one or the other category. Those who espouse the exemplar view argue that we reason from individual cases and not from abstract summaries.

We use both exemplar and prototypic representations (Smith, 1990). However, the distinction is an important one for social cognition. I had better categorize this man approaching me late at night on a darkened street, and do so quickly. Is he a thug? A harmless, pathetic, homeless person, perhaps a policeman? One way I might decide is to compare him to the prototype of a thug. And where in my limited experience do I get such a prototype? Why, from newspapers and accounts from others. In short, I may use a stereotype of a thug to make my judgement, On the other hand, if I use exemplars, my recent experiences may play a larger role. The man approaching is large, has a dark complexion, is dressed shabbily, but as I try to find exemplars of such men I have encountered recently, I keep coming up with men I have recently met at a local shelter for alcoholics.

## Memory

### Memory is selective

While there have been many debates about how memory works, there has been general agreement on several basic facts. Perhaps the most central fact of our memory systems is that they are selective. We do not see and hear everything around us, and do not place into our memory storage all the things that register. Clearly we do not and probably cannot remember everything we have seen or heard, and that is surely useful. Would you want to clutter up your mind with everything that happened to you yesterday?

Sometimes we have trouble remembering because the information we require was never stored effectively. When students take exams, they may find that information they have read was never really incorporated into their store of useful information. Sometimes we have trouble remembering things because we can't retrieve the information. You may, for example, have trouble remembering the name of a childhood friend at the moment, but find the name comes easily when you visit your parents or childhood hang-outs.

### Memory is biased

A second fact of memory is that it is sometimes not a faithful representation of experience. As we have suggested it leaves out many details that were never recorded or which have been forgotten. Beyond that, however, our memories are influenced by assumptions we make and inferences we draw. Having decided that the man before me is a criminal, I may remember him as bigger and more muscular than he really is.

Some of our "memories" are more or less conscious reconstructions of past events based on our schemata. So if I ask you what shoes you wore last Friday, you probably do not have a ready memory image at hand. However, you may reason that you wore your sneakers because you were shopping that day and you always wear sneakers to shop unless the weather is really bad.

However, even in cases where our memories are not based on conscious reconstructions, they may be biased by our knowledge about what we know must have happened. Research on eyewitness testimony has documented the fact that questions people are asked about events they have seen may bias what they remember (Loftus, 1979). For example, people who are asked how fast a car was going when it *smashed* into another car give higher estimates than those who are asked how fast the car was going when it *hit* the other car. We trust our memories (what other choice do we have?), but we should also be aware that they are sometimes wrong. In any event, we often remember information as particularly consistent with the schemata we used to understand and process that information.

## Memory for inconsistent information

Schema theories argue that we should best remember information consistent with our schemata. However, if you stop and think about it, our mental lives would be in sorry shape if all we did was remember the ways things are like they are supposed to be. Taken to the extreme we could never recall any new information. Suppose you have a conversation with a professor. You will note the ways in which she fits the stereotype (schema) you have for a professor, but is that all you remember? Surely you also recall some of the things that make her different from other professors you know. Indeed, there is now good evidence that we do recall especially well information that is inconsistent with our schemata and expectations (Stangor & McMillan, 1992). This, of course, allows us to individuate our experiences.

## Inferences

We all draw conclusions, lots of them, about what we have seen, heard, and remember. Because of our vast experience and many learning experiences, we all have a store of what might be called world-knowledge, that allows us to infer lots of things we never see. So at a party I normally assume that the people will understand my questions, that they have working hearts and auditory systems, and so on. This world knowledge is largely universal (at least within a given culture or group), and it represents the kinds of things we take for granted but which none the less guide our everyday behaviour at every step. I may also have more idiosyncratic knowledge that leads to other assumptions. I might assume that blond males who wear expensive suits have blue eyes and are taller than average; I may even assume that this blond man is less than optimally bright. I may assume that powerfully acting women are likely to be hard to talk to, that they will disdain my attempts at small talk, especially about sports.

These inferences are important inasmuch as they guide our interactions and our attempts to gather more information. If I assume that the blond man is deficient in IQ points I would initiate a conversation with him about the weather or vacations rather than the current state of the global warming controversy. I may, of course, be surprised to discover that he is a nuclear physicist. I may assume that the distinguished woman is also likely to be a business executive and interested in discussing the stock market only to discover that she is a famous cook or self-help author. Of course, sometimes our stereotypically guided inferences are perfectly accurate.

# CONCLUSIONS

Nothing is as important to most of us as other people and their behaviour. Unfortunately the importance of social stimuli is more than matched by their complexity. The behaviour of others is dynamic, and it not only changes according to its own rules but also is responsive to the behaviour of perceivers who often find themselves trying to understand behaviour that they, themselves, have an ongoing role in creating. Unfortunately, we are a long way from understanding how we accomplish simple cognitive tasks such as reading prose or recognizing physical objects and even further from knowing how we understand the much more complex social world around us. Yet since the 1960s we have not only dramatically increased our scientific knowledge about social cognition, but also learned exciting new ways of studying it. There is every reason to believe that the study of social cognition will remain central to social and cognitive psychology, and that we will continue to learn even more about its mysteries.

## FURTHER READING

Fiske, S. T., & Taylor S. E. (1991). *Social cognition* (2nd edn). New York: McGraw-Hill.

Hewstone, M. (1989). *Causal attribution: From cognitive processes to collective beliefs*. Oxford: Basil Blackwell.

Schneider, D. J., Hastorf, A. H., & Ellsworth, P. C. (1979). *Person perception* (2nd edn) Reading, MA: Addison-Wesley.

Uleman, J. S., & Bargh, J. A. (Eds) (1989). *Unintended thought*. New York: Guilford.

Wyer, R. S., Jr, & Srull, T. K. (1989). *Memory and cognition in its social context*. Hillsdale, NJ: Lawrence Erlbaum.

## REFERENCES

Anderson, N. H. (1981). *Foundations of information integration theory*. New York: Academic Press.

Bargh, J. A. (1989). Conditional automaticity: Varieties of automatic influence in social perception and cognition. In J. S. Uleman & J. A. Bargh (Eds) *Unintended thought* (pp. 3–51). New York: Guilford.

Bartlett, F. C. (1932). *Remembering: A study in experimental social psychology*. Cambridge: Cambridge University Press.

Brewer, M. C. (1988). A dual process model of impression formation. In T. K. Srull & R. S. Wyer, Jr, (Eds) *Advances in social cognition* (vol. 1, pp. 1–36). Hillsdale, NJ: Lawrence Erlbaum.

Cronbach, L. J. (1955). Processes affecting scores on "understanding of others" and "assumed similarity". *Psychological Bulletin*, *52*, 177–193.

Devine, P. G. (1989). Stereotypes and prejudice: Their automatic and controlled components. *Journal of Personality and Social Psychology*, *56*, 5–18.

Ekman, P., & Friesen, W. V. (1975). *Unmasking the face*. Englewood Cliffs, NJ: Prentice-Hall.

Fiedler, K., & Semin, G. (1988). On the causal information conveyed by different interpersonal verbs: The role of implicit sentence context. *Social Cognition*, *6*, 21–39.

Fiske, S. T., & Taylor, S. E. (1991). *Social cognition* (2nd edn). New York: McGraw-Hill.

Funder, D. C. (1987). Errors and mistakes: Evaluating the accuracy of social judgment. *Psychological Bulletin*, *101*, 75–90.

Gilbert, D. T. (1989). Thinking lightly about others: Automatic components of the social inference process. In J. S. Uleman & J. A. Bargh (Eds) *Unintended thought* (pp. 189–211). New York: Guilford.

Heider, F. (1958). *The psychology of interpersonal relations*. New York: Wiley.

Hewstone, M. (1989) *Causal attribution: From cognitive processes to collective beliefs*. Oxford: Basil Blackwell.

Hilton D. J., & Slugoski, B. R. (1986). *Knowledge-based causal attribution: The abnormal conditions focus model. Psychological Review*, *93*, 75–88.

Jaspars, J. M. F. (1983). The process of attribution in common sense In M. R. C. Hewstone (Ed.) *Attribution theory: Social and functional extensions* (pp. 28–44). Oxford: Basil Blackwell.

Jones, E. E., & Davis, K. E. (1965). From acts to dispositions: The attribution process in person perception. In L. Berkowitz (Ed.) *Advances in experimental social psychology* (vol. 2, pp. 219–276). New York: Academic Press.

Jones, E. E., & Nisbett, R. E. (1972). The actor and observer: Divergent perceptions of the causes of behavior. In E. E. Jones, D. Kanouse, H. H. Kelley, R. E. Nisbett, S. Valins, & B. Weiner (Eds) *Attribution: Perceiving the causes of behavior* (pp. 79–94). Morristown, NJ: General Learning Press.

Kelley, H. H. (1967). Attribution theory in social psychology. In *Nebraska Symposium on Motivation* (pp. 192–238). Lincoln, NB: University of Nebraska Press.

Lewicki, P. (1986). *Nonconscious social information processing*. New York: Academic Press.

Loftus, E. F. (1979). *Eyewitness testimony*. Cambridge, MA: Harvard University Press.

McGill, A. L. (1989). Context effects in judgments of causality. *Journal of Personality and Social Psychology*, *57*, 189–200.

Newman, L. S., & Uleman, J. S. (1989). Spontaneous trait inference. In J. S. Uleman & J. A. Bargh (Eds) *Unintended thought* (pp. 155–188). New York: Guilford.

Nisbett, R. E., & Wilson, T. D. (1977a). The halo effect: Evidence for unconscious alteration of judgments. *Journal of Personality and Social Psychology*, *35*, 250–256.

Nisbett, R. E., & Wilson, T. D. (1977b). Telling more than we can know: Verbal reports on mental processes. *Psychological Review*, *84*, 231–259.

Ostrom, T. M. (1984). The sovereignty of social cognition. In R. S. Wyer & T. K. Srull (Eds) *Handbook of social cognition* (vol. 1, pp. 1–38). Hillsdale, NJ: Lawrence Erlbaum.

Park, B., & Judd, C. M. (1989). Agreement on initial impressions: Differences due to perceivers, trait dimensions, and target behaviors. *Journal of Personality and Social Psychology*, *56*, 493–505.

Rosch, E. H. (1978). Principles of categorization. In E. Rosch & B. B. Lloyd (Eds) *Cognition and categorization* (pp. 28–48). Hillsdale, NJ: Lawrence Erlbaum.

Schneider, D. J. (1973). Implicit personality theory. *Psychological Bulletin*, *79*, 294–309.

Schneider, D. J. (1991). Social cognition. *Annual Review of Psychology*, *42*, 527–561.

Schneider, D. J., Hastorf, A. H., & Ellsworth, P. C. (1979). *Person perception* (2nd edn) Reading, MA: Addison-Wesley.

Skowronski, J. J., & Carlston, D. E. (1989). Negativity and extremity biases in impression formation: A review of explanations. *Psychological Bulletin*, *105*, 131–142.

Slovic, P., Fischhoff, B., & Lichtenstein, S. (1982). Facts versus fears: Understanding perceived risk. In D. Kahneman, P. Slovic, & A. Tversky (Eds) *Judgment under uncertainty: Heuristics and biases* (pp. 463–489). Cambridge: Cambridge University Press.

Smith, E. R. (1990). Content and process specificity in the effects of prior experiences. In T. K. Srull & R. S. Wryer, Jr (Eds) *Advances in social cognition* (vol. 3, pp. 1–91). Hillsdale, NJ: Lawrence Erlbaum.

Stangor, C., & McMillan, D. (1992). Memory for expectancy-congruent and expectancy-incongruent information: A review of the social and social developmental literatures. *Psychological Bulletin*, *111*, 42–61.

Swann, W. B., Jr (1984). Quest for accuracy in person perception: A matter of pragmatics. *Psychological Review*, *91*, 457–477.

Taft, R. (1955). The ability to judge people. *Psychological Bulletin*, *52*, 1–23.

Trope, Y. (1986). Identification and inferential processes in dispositional attribution. *Psychological Review*, *93*, 239–257.

Turnbull, W., & Slugoski, B. R. (1988). Conversational and linguistic processes in causal attribution. In D. J. Hilton (Ed.) *Contemporary science and natural explanation: Commonsense perceptions of causality* (pp. 66–93). Brighton: Harvester.

Tversky, A., & Kahneman, D. (1974). Judgment under uncertainty: Heuristics and biases. *Science*, *185*, 1124–1131.

Van Kleeck, M., Hillger, L., & Brown, R. (1988). Pitting verbal schemes against information variables in attribution. *Social Cognition*, *6*, 89–106.

Watson, D. (1989). Strangers' ratings of the five robust personality factors: Evidence of a surprising convergence with self-report. *Journal of Personality and Social Psychology*, *57*, 120–128.

# 4

# PREJUDICE AND INTERGROUP CONFLICT

## *James Vivian and Rupert Brown*
### *University of Kent, England*

---

**Prejudice as a feature of
individual psychology**
The prejudiced personality
Belief similarity as an
　explanation of prejudice
Frustration, aggression, and
　prejudice
Individual cognitive processes
　underlying prejudice
**Prejudice as a result of
intergroup relationships**

Relative deprivation
Realistic conflict theory
**Prejudice as an aspect of group
membership**
Social identity theory
**Reducing prejudice**
**Conclusion**
**Further reading**
**References**

---

Although there has been little discernible improvement in social relations across the globe, there have been considerable advances in our understanding of the causes of prejudice and intergroup conflict. In analysing the major contributions of social psychology to this topic it is possible to distinguish between three approaches: there are those that locate the cause of prejudice in the psychological make-up of the individual; there are approaches that emphasise the role that external or environmental factors play; and finally, there are approaches in which group membership itself is seen as critically important. Each of these different perspectives may be important to a full understanding of the causes of intergroup conflict and prejudice and the best strategies for their reduction.

　By prejudice we mean the derogatory attitudes that members of one group

57

may hold about another, and the discriminatory behaviour that is often associated with this. Although prejudice and intergroup conflict are conceptually distinct, they often coexist; wherever we find prejudice, we also find conflict, if only dormant. Prejudice, then, can be thought of as a special case of intergroup conflict.

Intergroup conflict occurs when people think or behave antagonistically towards another group or its members in terms of their group memberships and seem motivated by concerns relating to those groups (Sherif, 1966; Tajfel & Turner, 1986). Conversely, conflict is "interpersonal" to the extent that no reference to membership is made, and the issues dividing the participants are specific to those particular individuals. The distinction between these levels of social interaction is critical as behaviour is often qualitatively different between intergroup and interpersonal contexts. In spite of this dichotomy, most social relationships are recognized to be a mixture of both interpersonal and intergroup components, the relative importance of which may fluctuate over time and across situations.

## PREJUDICE AS A FEATURE OF INDIVIDUAL PSYCHOLOGY

### The prejudiced personality

Some psychologists believe that people who display prejudice differ in personality from non-prejudiced people. This notion was popularized by Adorno, Frenkel-Brunswick, Levinson, and Sanford (1950) in their analysis of the "authoritarian personality". These authors argued that a particularly strict upbringing by parents overly concerned with convention and conformity gives rise to an authoritarian personality, which is thought to predispose certain people to prejudice. According to this theory, the hostility felt towards such parents is repressed by the child, who then idealizes the parents and who subsequently displays a deferential and submissive attitude towards authority figures in general (who are presumed to symbolize the parents). Following from a presumed need to discharge the psychic energy that has accumulated from repression, the pent-up hostility is displaced on to less threatening, lower status targets who are normally other groups (e.g., foreigners, minority groups). These are seen as inherently defective or flawed in character and therefore deserving of contempt.

To measure authoritarianism, Adorno et al. (1950) developed the F-scale (tendency towards Fascism scale). Through detailed clinical interviews and projective tests of personality, Adorno and his colleagues were able to examine the relationships between F-scale responses, patterns of personality, and upbringing. Consistent with their theorizing, results seemed to indicate that highly authoritarian individuals tended to hold more ethnocentric (e.g., anti-Semitic, racist) attitudes and tended also to be those who had been subjected to stricter child-rearing practices than their less authoritarian counterparts.

Following its publication, critics pointed to methodological flaws associated with the F-scale and the clinical interviews used to validate it (Brown, 1965). The major problem with the F-scale is that the items are coded in such a way that agreement with statements always implies an authoritarian attitude of one form or another (see Table 1). As a result, it is unclear whether those who score highly on the F-scale are actually more authoritarian than others or whether they are simply more inclined towards acquiescence with statements in general. Further, the clinical interviews used to validate the F-scale as a measure of authoritarianism were flawed because the interviewers were aware of the prior F-scale responses of their interviewees, thus possibly contaminating the interview in subtle ways.

But perhaps a more damning criticism of the theory relates to the problems associated with an "individual differences" (i.e., personality) approach to explaining prejudice and intergroup behaviour (Billig, 1976). The problem, very simply, is that an analysis of individual personalities cannot account for the large-scale social behaviour that normally characterizes prejudice and intergroup conflict more generally. If it were true that prejudice derived from a disorder in personality, then we would expect the expression of prejudice or discrimination within groups to vary as much as the personalities of members comprising the group. But in fact the evidence seems to indicate that prejudice within groups is often remarkably uniform. For example, Pettigrew (1958), while studying prejudice in South Africa and the United States, found that levels of prejudice between the countries differed markedly while

*Table 1* Sample items from the F-scale

1 Obedience and respect for authority are the most important virtues that children should learn.
2 Young people sometimes get rebellious ideas, but as they grow up they ought to get over them and settle down.
3 What the youth needs most is strict discipline, rugged determination, and the will to work and fight for family and country.
4 An insult to our honour should always be punished.
5 Sex crimes, such as rape and attacks on children, deserve more than mere imprisonment; such criminals ought to be publicly whipped, or worse.
6 A person who has bad manners, habits, and breeding can hardly expect to get along with decent people.
7 Most of our social problems would be solved if we could somehow get rid of the immoral, crooked, and feeble-minded people.
8 If people would talk less and work more, everybody would be better off.
9 People can be divided into two distinct classes: the weak and the strong.
10 Human nature being what it is, there will always be war and conflict.

*Source*: Adorno, Frenkel-Brunswick, Levinson, and Sanford, 1950, pp. 255–257

levels of authoritarianism did not. As a result, he concluded that rather than seeing the prejudice as an expression of a personality disorder, it was more likely to be a result of the norms prevailing in society. The fact that all members are exposed to such cultural norms may thus account for the oft-observed uniformity of prejudice.

Additionally, if prejudice is rooted in individual personalities, which are, by definition, enduring characteristics, then one would expect consistency over time in the expression of prejudice. But the historical evidence seems to reveal patterns of prejudice that suddenly appear and disappear, depending on the relations between the groups in question. Thus, for example, the prejudice displayed by Americans during the Second World War that eventually led to the internment of thousands of Japanese living in the United States cannot plausibly be explained by the individual personalities of Americans suddenly becoming more authoritarian in the 1940s. It seems more likely that the rise in prejudice directed specifically at the Japanese was related to the change in the objective relations between the groups that followed the bombing of Pearl Harbor.

## Belief similarity as an explanation of prejudice

As an alternative to a "personality explanation" of prejudice, Rokeach (1960) offered an account that emphasized the role of belief systems. He proposed that similarity or "congruence" of individuals' beliefs determine, in large part, their attitudes towards one another. Specifically, he reasoned that we are generally more attracted to those who share our beliefs and opinions because they validate and legitimize our own. Those who disagree with us, on the other hand, are less attractive because they invalidate our beliefs.

Rokeach made a direct application of these ideas to racial prejudice. According to belief congruence theory, racial prejudice is seen as an outcome of perceived differences in belief (belief incongruence) between members of different racial groups and, further, that these belief differences are ultimately more important than the differences in group membership. Thus, according to Rokeach, we are more likely to discriminate against someone in our own ethnic group who disagrees with us than against someone in another group with whom we concur.

In order to test the theory, Rokeach, Smith, and Evans (1960) developed what has come to be called the "Race-belief" paradigm whereby individual subjects are presented with "stimulus persons" who vary in terms of their attitudinal and ethnic similarity to the subject. With few exceptions, studies utilizing this paradigm have generally established that belief influences subjects' reported attitudes more than race. Thus, white subjects are usually more attracted to a black person with similar beliefs than a white person with different beliefs (Insko, Nacoste, & Moe, 1983). Field research has also provided results generally supportive of belief congruence theory. Other researchers, working in different cultural contexts, report relatively strong correlations between perceived cultural or linguistic similarity and attraction to different ethnic groups (e.g., Berry, Kalin, & Taylor, 1977; Brewer & Campbell, 1976).

As a further test of the hypothesized connection between similarity and intergroup attitudes, a number of experimental investigations have been conducted using methods that do not pit belief similarity directly against group membership. The evidence on this front is somewhat mixed. While certain studies offer support for the idea that similar outgroups are treated better than dissimilar ones (e.g., Brown, 1984), others do not (Diehl, 1988). In fact, there is some experimental evidence that actually contradicts belief congruence theory. Under certain conditions, such as where there is strong attitudinal consensus in the ingroup, unstable status discrepancies, or competition between groups, more discrimination can be found against a similar outgroup (Brown, 1984). These latter experimental findings thus challenge some of Rokeach's original claims.

How can these disparate results be accounted for? One explanation is offered by Brown and Turner (1981), who caution against the direct application of ideas developed to explain interpersonal behaviour to the realm of intergroup relations which are controlled, they argue, by different psychological processes. In a reconsideration of the race-belief literature, for example, they suggest that race may have had little impact because of the explicitly interpersonal, as opposed to intergroup, nature of the encounter. When race is made salient, they argue, the findings can be reversed, with race influencing judgements more than similarity. This argument has been supported by an experiment in which either interpersonal or intergroup similarity was made the main focus of people's attention (Diehl, 1988). As expected, in the former case, less discrimination was observed while the latter condition led to an increase in ingroup favouritism.

As a complete explanation of intergroup prejudice, then, belief-congruence theory is probably inadequate in its original form. In fact, Rokeach himself recognized the limitations of the theory and limited his claims to situations where prejudice or racism is not institutionalized as it was in South Africa under apartheid or where there is not significant social support for their expression (e.g., in certain areas in the southern United States).

### Frustration, aggression, and prejudice

Predating both the authoritarian personality and belief-similarity theories was an ambitious attempt by Dollard, Doob, Miller, Mowrer, and Sears (1939) to explain aggressive behaviour between individuals and groups in society. Combining insights from traditional psychoanalytic and learning theories, Dollard et al. proposed that frustration, deriving from the blocking of basic needs, produces a "build-up of psychic energy" or an "instigation to aggress". Following a hydraulic model of human personality, such mounting pressure is alleged to be experienced as an aversive state of arousal that must eventually be relieved. Release of this energy restores balance or equilibrium and is thereby experienced as pleasurable or "cathartic". According to the theory, the release of such mounting tension normally takes the form of explicit or implicit acts of aggression that may be directed at the original source of the frustration or at alternative targets. Dollard and colleagues point out that the source of the frustration is often seen as relatively powerful or threatening (e.g., parents) and is sometimes difficult to identify at all, as when the impoverished consider the causes of their unfortunate position. Borrowing another psychoanalytic concept, Dollard et al. suggested that in cases like these, the aggression is displaced on to alternative targets who either share some surface similarity to the threatening source or are simply convenient scapegoats.

Dollard et al. (1939) used these ideas to explain prejudice, believing that they could account for both the pervasive character of prejudice and its apparent historical specificity. Prejudice is pervasive, they argued, because frustration is pervasive. In every culture at any point in time, most individuals are not having all of their needs met to their satisfaction. They may feel economically disadvantaged or unhappy with work or family life, but because almost nobody is perfectly contented, there exists at all times and places a certain "baseline" level of frustration and, consequently, of aggression. And because the sources of such frustration endemic to social life cannot be easily identified, the associated aggression is thereby displaced on to convenient targets, the targets of prejudice who are normally relatively powerless minority groups. Historical fluctuations can be explained, according to the theory, in terms of the frustrations associated with changing economic conditions (e.g., the rise of anti-Semitism in Germany following the First World War may have been due to the collapse of the German economy at this time). Evidence in support of this idea was offered by Hovland and Sears (1940) among others, who showed that lynchings of blacks in the southern United States in the late nineteenth and early twentieth centuries were related to the price of cotton, a major industry in this region during that time. As the economic standing of many declined along with the price of cotton, the number of lynchings increased. Presumably, the bleak economy produced feelings of frustration in those affected who vented their frustration in a particularly savage way on the convenient scapegoats of the day, the blacks. Some experimental studies have lent further support to the theory (e.g., Miller & Bugelski, 1948).

Despite its attractive simplicity and its empirical support, frustration-aggression theory may still be limited in its ability to explain intergroup prejudice. As with personality, the level of frustration experienced may vary from individual to individual and thus one would expect more variation in the expression of aggression or prejudice than is normally observed. Another major limitation relates to the choice of particular outgroups as targets of prejudice. Why, for example, did whites in the United States select blacks for lynchings rather than other disadvantaged minority groups? Finally, it has been established that frustration was neither necessary nor sufficient to produce aggression leading to a reformulation of the original theory (Berkowitz, 1962). However, even this revised version, based as it is on individual motivational states, is subject to some of the same criticisms that applied to the original theory offered by Dollard et al. (1939).

## Individual cognitive processes underlying prejudice

Some theories of prejudice emphasize the role of cognitive processes in the formation and maintenance of negative group stereotypes. Stereotypes are preconceived ideas about entire classes of people and are thought to derive more from limitations in the ability to process information than from a disordered personality or individual needs or motivations. According to Tajfel (1959), we need to simplify the extraordinarily complex physical and social world that we inhabit by placing objects, events, and people (including the self) into various categories. Following from such categorical differentiation, Tajfel further showed that differences between separate categories of physical stimuli are overestimated (Tajfel & Wilkes, 1963). Similar effects have been obtained with social stimuli (people). Using children from Switzerland as subjects, Doise, Deschamps, and Meyer (1978) demonstrated how groups of boys and girls perceived greater differences between photographs of unknown boys and girls when the gender distinction was made explicit than when it was not. Further, the photographs of boys alone and girls alone were judged to be more similar under these same conditions. These results were repeated in a second study which involved judgements of Swiss linguistic groups. Thus, Doise et al. (1987) showed that both differences between and similarities within social categories are accentuated when intergroup categorizations are clear.

It is important to note, however, that the effects of social categorization are not symmetrical. While it appears that categorical distinctions tend to enhance the perception of within-category similarity, this effect is normally more pronounced for the outgroup which is seen as more internally homogeneous than the ingroup (e.g., Quattrone, 1986). For example, Jones, Wood, and Quattrone (1981) found when they asked members of university clubs to estimate the variability (of personalities) of members belonging to different clubs, that club members consistently perceived other clubs as more homogeneous than their own. With some important exceptions (e.g., Simon & Brown, 1987), similar results have been obtained in diverse contexts generally confirming the idea that group members tend to believe while "they" are all the same, "we" are different.

The cognitive process of social categorization may also lie at the heart of stereotype formation. It has been shown that when two distinctive (unusual) events co-occur, people come to believe that there is a correlation between them and that they go together (Chapman & Chapman, 1967). Hamilton and Gifford (1976) extended this notion to stereotypes by arguing, for example, that whites might perceive a correlation between criminality and black skin colour because the two events are unusual and therefore distinctive. To demonstrate this, they presented subjects with scenarios depicting desirable and undesirable actions of members of hypothetical groups. While one of the groups was twice as large as the other and, overall, there were more desirable than undesirable acts depicted, the proportion of desirable to undesirable behaviour within each group was held constant. So, for example, although there were twice as many undesirable acts emanating from the larger group, there were also twice as many people in that group, so there was no actual correlation between the nature of the act (desirable or undesirable) and group membership. Nevertheless, when asked to indicate which acts came from the larger and smaller groups, subjects overestimated the number of undesirable (less common) behaviours in the smaller (minority) group (see Table 2). Consistent with Hamilton's reasoning on the impact of distinctive stimuli, subjects thus perceived an "illusory correlation" between the possession of undesirable traits and minority group membership. This research provides some support, then, for the notion that distinctiveness explains why minorities are seen as having undesirable traits.

Although there is some evidence that people hold fewer derogatory stereotypes about traditionally oppressed groups than before (e.g., Campbell, 1971) later evidence seems to suggest that stereotypes persist even among liberally minded people. When more subtle measures are used (Crosby, Bromley, & Saxe, 1980) or when discriminatory attitudes cannot be unambiguously attributed to prejudice (Gaertner & Dovidio, 1986), a surprising

*Table 2* Distinctive (infrequent) events as a source of illusory correlation

|  | Group | |
|  | A (majority) | B (minority) |
| --- | --- | --- |
| Actual distribution of behaviours between two groups | | |
| Desirable | 18 (67%) | 9 (33%) |
| Undesirable | 8 (67%) | 4 (33%) |
| Distribution of behaviours between two groups as perceived by subjects | | |
| Desirable | 17.5 (65%) | 9.5 (35%) |
| Undesirable | 5.8 (48%) | 6.2 (52%) |

*Source*: Hamilton and Gifford, 1976, table 1
*Note*: Subjects overestimate the amount of undesirable behaviour emanating from the smaller (minority) group (Group B)

number of seemingly non-prejudiced people behave in characteristically prejudiced ways. Why is it that stereotypes are so resistant to change? One possibility is that people selectively attend to information that confirms their stereotypes. Thus, for example, Howard and Rothbart (1980) showed that even when ingroup and outgroup speakers make the same number of favourable and unfavourable remarks, subjects recall more unfavourable remarks coming from the outgroup. This selective memory together with the fact that unfavourable stereotypes are generally easier to acquire but more difficult to lose than favourable ones, probably contributes to the persistence of unflattering stereotypes of minority groups (Rothbart & Park, 1986).

Additionally, there is reason to believe that many of these cognitive processes may be outside of conscious control. Devine (1989) has proposed that most people share a knowledge of stereotypes and that this knowledge can affect, quite unconsciously, the processing of information. In one study Devine showed that a hypothetical person was viewed as more hostile (black stereotype) by subjects (both prejudiced and non-prejudiced) who had been previously exposed to stereotype-relevant words flashed so quickly that subjects could not recall their content. Presumably, the presentation of the stereotype-associated words activated the cultural stereotype which then had unconscious effects on subjects' assessments of the hypothetical person.

Although there is good reason to believe that individual cognitive processes play a role in the formation and maintenance of stereotypes, there is still reason to doubt that they can account for all of the stereotypes that we hold. If it were true, for example, that people tend to exaggerate the correlation between unusual events that sometimes co-occur, then minority groups should have as part of their stereotype both undesirable and unusually desirable traits (e.g., geniuses). Clearly, this is not the case as stereotypes of minority groups are normally derogatory. This fact highlights one of the important limitations of the purely cognitive explanation of prejudice phenomena: it cannot explain why categorical differentiation normally takes on an asymmetry that either favours the ingroup or derogates the outgroup. In addition, cognitive explanations are still individualistic in nature and thus have difficulty explaining widespread, collective behaviour which, it can be argued, are controlled by processes that differ from those operating at the individual psychological level.

## PREJUDICE AS A RESULT OF INTERGROUP RELATIONSHIPS

### Relative deprivation

Frustration-aggression theory subsequently evolved into a form which was more explicitly "intergroup" in focus and thus overcame some of the difficulties associated with the earlier version. Following Berkowitz's (1962) lead in emphasizing the subjective nature of frustration, others have argued that it is precisely when people feel deprived of something that they feel entitled to that they experience frustration. The discrepancy between our actual attainments (e.g., position in life) and our expectations (e.g., the position we feel we deserve) is referred to as "relative deprivation". Two types of relative deprivation can be distinguished (Runciman, 1966). One is "egoistic" relative deprivation which derives from comparisons made with other individuals who are seen as similar to oneself. Thus, if colleagues or peers are considerably better off in terms of wages or standard of living, one would be expected to feel deprived relative to these similar others. In "fraternalistic" relative deprivation, on the other hand, feelings of deprivation are thought to derive from comparisons between groups such as when members of particular ethnic or minority groups consider their standard of living in comparison to the dominant majority.

Runciman's discovery that intergroup comparisons could lead to relative deprivation has been confirmed in a number of studies. Vanneman and Pettigrew (1972) found that racist political attitudes were related to feelings of relative deprivation generally and that the most racist attitudes were found among those who reported being fraternally deprived. Further demonstrating the utility of distinguishing between egoistic and fraternalistic deprivation, Abeles (1976) and Walker and Mann (1987) have shown that blacks in the United States and unemployed workers in Australia were more likely to engage in social action when they felt that their group as a whole has not attained what they justly deserved relative to other groups. Abeles also points out that levels of militancy appear to be highest among blacks with higher socio-economic and educational status. This is consistent with Runciman's observation that leaders of collective movements are usually the least deprived members of their groups in an objective sense. Following from an understanding of frustration as a subjective phenomenon, it is likely that these individuals have higher expectations both for themselves and for their group and thus experience the perceived deprivation more acutely.

Relative deprivation theory is thus quite helpful in explaining when hostility will emerge between groups. When members of a given social group perceive a discrepancy between what they believe their group deserves and what they have actually attained, members share a sense of deprivation and a sense of injustice. Because notions of justice are socially determined in the sense that they reflect norms and values of a given culture, they are thought to apply equally across all members of the group. The shared sense of injustice then helps explain the uniformity of behaviour that normally characterizes intergroup relations generally and prejudice in particular.

## Realistic conflict theory

Social scientists in various disciplines have long recognized that in addition to the needs, desires, or personalities of individual members, the goals or interests of groups are potent influences of behaviour. Thus, when members believe that another group can satisfy its desires only at their own group's expense (and vice versa), hostility develops between the groups along with the discriminatory and prejudiced behaviour that is commonly associated with such antagonistic intergroup relationships. According to this view, the attitudes and actions of members of different groups reflect the goal relations between those groups. This approach to intergroup relations is known as realistic conflict theory, as real (or perceived) conflicts of interest are presumed to underlie much of the prejudice and hostility often observed between groups.

The best known proponents of this approach have been Muzafer Sherif and his colleagues, who conducted some of the earliest empirical investigations of intergroup conflict. In these studies, they noted the relative ease with which groups of otherwise healthy, well-adjusted boys could be induced to display marked ingroup favouritism and openly hostile behaviour towards other groups of boys, simply as a result of introducing a competition between them (Sherif, 1966). Furthermore, they were able to reduce the tension by replacing the competitive arrangement, whereby one group succeeded at the other's expense, with a cooperative one, where both groups' success was contingent on cooperation between the groups. Based on these and other observations, Sherif suggested that conflict between groups, and the associated intergroup biases, develops through competition and can be reduced through intergroup cooperation in pursuit of superordinate goals.

Results similar to Sherif's have also been obtained among groups of adult managers in human relations workshops and among members of different cultures (e.g., Blake & Mouton, 1962; Diab, 1970). Nevertheless, subsequently, findings have begun to accumulate which suggest that while competition may be *sufficient for* the emergence of intergroup bias, it may not be *necessary*. In a series of what have come to be called "minimal group" experiments, where distinctions between groups are trivial (e.g., presumed aesthetic preferences) and members remain anonymous, the tendency to favour the ingroup either in evaluative judgements or the distribution of rewards has been clearly demonstrated (Rabbie & Horwitz, 1969; Tajfel, Flament, Billig, & Bundy, 1971). Additionally, though cooperative contact between groups in pursuit of "superordinate" goals generally improves relations between them, there are important exceptions when this is apparently not the case. For example, later research found that in order for the superordinate goals strategy to be effective, the cooperative effort must be successful and members of the groups must be able to preserve distinctive identities rather than being absorbed into a common culture (Brown & Wade, 1987; Worchel, Andreoli, & Folger, 1977). Otherwise, there is reason to believe that such contact can exacerbate rather than alleviate hostility.

# PREJUDICE AS AN ASPECT OF GROUP MEMBERSHIP

## Social identity theory

How can the "incipient hostility" that appears to emerge between groups even in the absence of explicit competition or conflicts of interest be explained? Further, why are comparisons between groups' material outcomes apparently so important in generating resentment and hostility? One influential theory which has been offered to explain these phenomena is one that emphasizes the role of cognitive and motivational processes in prejudice and intergroup relations; this explanation is now commonly known as social identity theory (Tajfel, 1978; Tajfel & Turner, 1986).

This theory starts with the assumption that the desire to understand and to evaluate oneself constitutes a primary motive underlying much of social behaviour. Joining two traditions in psychology, it proposes that we satisfy this desire through social categorization and social comparison. With social categorization, as noted, the complex social world is simplified by placing people, including the self, into various categories (e.g., gender, race, nationality, or political ideology). It is this process of self-categorization that defines what Tajfel called the social identity. Social identity theory hypothesizes that people are strongly motivated to understand and evaluate these group-based identities and, echoing an earlier theory (Festinger, 1954), it holds that this evaluative activity is primarily carried out through comparisons with other groups.

However, along with a need for self-evaluation and understanding, there may be a need for "self-enhancement". This added feature is necessary because while the dual processes of social categorization and social comparison can account for the tendency to compare and contrast groups, they cannot easily explain why, when the self is involved, the differentiation normally takes on an asymmetry that favours the groups to which one belongs (the ingroup). With this added concern for self-enhancement, it is argued that individuals are motivated not only by the desire to know and evaluate themselves, but also to evaluate themselves favourably relative to others. Comparisons between groups therefore often have the objective of attaining some distinctiveness from other groups in order to achieve or maintain a positive social identity. From this perspective, then, prejudice may be an expression of a basic motivation for a positive identity which is accomplished, in part, by positively distinguishing an ingroup from an outgroup.

There is abundant research evidence supporting the general claims of social identity theory. It is clear from the literature that intergroup bias (the tendency to favour the group to which one belongs over other groups) is an extraordinarily robust phenomenon which occurs in diverse contexts across a variety of group tasks (see Brewer, 1979). Consistent with the notion that people are motivated to attain positive social identities through intergroup comparisons, the evidence indicates that once groups are perceived to be meaningfully distinct from one another, intergroup bias often ensues in the form of discriminatory reward allocations, trait evaluations, or performance evaluations. In minimal group experiments especially, where the basis for group categorization is trivial, the results reveal a consistent pattern of ingroup favouritism in the allocation of financial rewards that supports social identity theory. Even when alternative allocation strategies would have yielded higher profits for an anonymous ingroup member, participants in these experiments tended to prefer strategies that maximized the difference between the groups' outcomes in favour of the ingroup (Tajfel et al., 1971; see also Figure 1). Similar results were obtained in a field setting where Brown (1978) noted factory-workers' desire to maintain wage differentials between their own and other departments even at the expense of their own absolute wage levels.

Central to social identity theory is the idea that group members discriminate against outsiders in the service of the need to achieve, maintain, or enhance self-esteem. The evidence that relates to this hypothesis is mixed. Consistent with this idea, Oakes and Turner (1980) found that group members who were given the opportunity to discriminate reported higher levels of self-esteem afterwards than those who could not discriminate. Nevertheless, other evidence on this front indicates that the relationship between self-esteem and intergroup behaviour is not as straightforward as social identity theory would predict. In some cases, higher levels of self-esteem are associated with intergroup discrimination while in others, discrimination is actually associated with lower levels of self-esteem (Abrams & Hogg, 1988). Another problem for the theory stems from the supposed link between the strength of group identification and the amount of intergroup bias. While many studies report a consistent relationship between identification and intergroup bias, the magnitude of the relationships are relatively weak, and, in some cases, they are actually negative (see Hinkle & Brown, 1990). Additionally, it is clear that in certain cases, people favour the outgroup. It is commonly found, for example, that members of low-status

| Ingroup member | 7 | 8 | 9 | 10 | 11 | 12 | 13 | 14 | 15 | 16 | 17 | 18 | 19 |
|---|---|---|---|---|---|---|---|---|---|---|---|---|---|
| Outgroup member | 1 | 3 | 5 | 7 | 9 | 11 | 13 | 15 | 17 | 19 | 21 | 23 | 25 |

*Figure 1* Sample matrix used in Tajfel et al. (1971). Subjects were instructed to allocate points (representing money) to anonymous members of their own and another group. Average responses were slightly to the left of the centre column (13, 13) suggesting that subjects were interested in allocating *more* money to the ingroup than to the outgroup member even at the expense of absolute profit for the ingroup member

groups exhibit outgroup favouritism to high-status outgroups (Mullen, Brown, & Smith, 1992). This does not fit simply with the theory's view that group members are attempting to create positive social identities by always engaging in ingroup-favouring behaviour.

Finally, and perhaps most importantly, it is not entirely clear whether social identity theory can account for intergroup prejudice if prejudice is defined as derogatory attitudes or behaviour directed at members of another group. Where the data are available, the majority of empirical studies concerned with intergroup bias report that differences in evaluations of ingroup and outgroup typically result from elevated ratings of the ingroup (Brewer, 1979). So while it is clear that members of groups often show favouritism to the group to which they belong, there is actually very little evidence that they derogate outgroups in the way that is characteristic of prejudice.

## REDUCING PREJUDICE

The various approaches discussed above have direct implications for the reduction of prejudice and the resolution of conflict. The majority of programmes aimed at fostering harmonious relations between previously conflictual groups have operated under assumptions embodied in what has come to be known as the "contact hypothesis" (Allport, 1954). This hypothesis asserts attitudes and behaviour towards outgroups will become more positive after interaction with them. Although many studies conducted in diverse contexts support this idea, because many others were less encouraging, several qualifications to the original hypothesis were required. Thus, the effects of contact are greatly enhanced if it is sanctioned by institutional supports (e.g., law, custom), takes place between participants on an equal status footing in pursuit of common goals, and provided it is of a sort that leads to the perception of communality between the two groups (Amir, 1969).

In spite of the early awareness that these moderating conditions were necessary for the success of intergroup contact, many integration policies in the United States and elsewhere have gone forward somewhat blindly, ignoring the recommendations of social scientists. Contact between black and white children in US public (state) schools is a case in point. Early legislative action imposing desegregation was largely ineffective in the reduction of prejudice between these children probably because the interracial contact in the school setting did not satisfy the criteria necessary for successful intergroup contact. The contact was mostly involuntary and of a superficial nature between groups of markedly different statuses in communities which were often unsupportive of the contact to begin with (Schofield, 1986). Another interesting example of an attempt to reduce ethnic prejudice was described by Schwarzwald and Amir (1984). This study is concerned with efforts in Israel to deal with inter-ethnic tensions between those of middle eastern (North African and Asian) and western (European and American) descent; it documents an "asymmetry" in the patterns of acceptance and rejection between members of these two cultural groups. When asked to indicate social preferences, for example, westerners of all ages tended to accept and prefer other westerners over their eastern counterparts. At the same time, those of eastern descent appear also to prefer westerners, devaluing their own cultural heritage and social standing. This situation is not unlike some encounters between black and white Americans where it has been established that sometimes the minority group (blacks) adopt the majority evaluation of their group and consider themselves less worthy (Clark & Clark, 1947). As in the United States, the results of imposed ethnic integration within the Israeli schools were not very encouraging primarily because policy was rarely guided by scientific knowledge. Because the schools continued to "track" (i.e., to stream) their students, the clear status differentials remained, leaving a disproportionate number of middle easterners in the lower tracks (Schwarzwald & Amir, 1984).

These examples in the United States and Israel strongly suggest that contact itself is largely ineffective at reducing prejudice between cultural groups. More recent theoretical work has built on the original contact hypothesis in specifying additional conditions under which contact will successfully reduce prejudice and thereby improve relations between groups. It is generally agreed that intergroup contact is successful to the extent that diverse groups can coexist peacefully while maintaining distinctive identities. Such integration is the goal in any truly pluralistic society and should be distinguished from assimilation, another possible outcome of contact which is said to have occurred when previously differentiated groups are reduced into a common culture. In spite of efforts in numerous experimental and societal contexts, however, it remains to be seen how best to realize the goal of true integration.

To this end, two seemingly divergent positions have been advanced, both of which claim to offer the optimal strategy for facilitating integration between groups (Brewer and Miller, 1984; Hewstone & Brown, 1986). In their model of "de-categorization" Brewer and Miller propose that the goal of contact is "non-category-based" interaction. The major symptoms of category-based interaction, which prevents integration, include the depersonalization of outgroup members, who are treated as if they are part of a homogeneous or undifferentiated category. In order to achieve more harmonious relations, it follows that respective group memberships need to be made less salient during contact, the boundaries between groups less rigid, and social relations more interpersonally oriented. The assumption is that repeated interpersonal contact with members of the disliked group will produce stereotype-disconfirming experiences which encourage truly interpersonal as opposed to intergroup interactions. Miller, Brewer, and Edwards (1985) have provided some experimental evidence in favour of this approach.

71

They found that cooperative group interactions which emphasized interpersonal (rather than task) aspects of the situation generated more favourable intergroup attitudes and less discriminatory reward allocations.

Consistent with this view, several educational interventions have been developed which attempt to structure intergroup contact in a way that will weaken boundaries between groups by providing members with cooperative interpersonal experiences with members of a disliked group. One application of this strategy was offered by Aronson and his colleagues in their work with school-aged children of varying ethnic backgrounds in the United States (Aronson, Blaney, Stephan, Sikes, & Snapp, 1978). They devised a cooperative learning strategy referred to as the "jigsaw classroom". Classrooms employing this technique are comprised of racially mixed groups of students who are each responsible for mastering separate portions of material and for teaching this material to others in their group. Members thus depend on one another to achieve the common or superordinate goal of getting good marks in the class. Evidence indicates that students in jigsaw classes report liking classmates of other races more after the technique has been introduced than before. More generally, curricula which emphasize cooperative learning strategies seem to be effective in reducing intergroup tensions (Slavin, 1983).

The problem with many of these strategies that draw attention away from group memberships is that positive attitude changes are often restricted to the situation that produced them and to the members present in the original contact situation. Although the contact may provide stereotype-disconfirming experiences, the individuals present can be considered atypical or exceptions to the rule with respect to the group as a whole. As a result, attitudinal and behavioural changes achieved in the contact situation are often short-lived.

Hewstone and Brown (1986) addressed this problem of the lack of generalization associated with many intergroup contact efforts. Their model is based on the distinction between interpersonal and intergroup behaviour. Because the two levels of interaction may be controlled by different psychological processes, they argue that contact will produce generalized attitude change beyond the contact setting only when the interaction is construed as intergroup in nature, when members are seen as representative of their respective groups. In an experimental context, Wilder (1984) provided evidence in favour of this model. By varying the level of "prototypicality" of an outgroup member, he found that significant improvements in the evaluation of the outgroup as a whole, in this case a rival college, occurred only when there was a pleasant encounter with what was perceived to be a typical member of the outgroup (see Figure 2). In this case, a stereotype-confirming, yet pleasant experience with a typical outgroup member improved perceptions of rival groups.

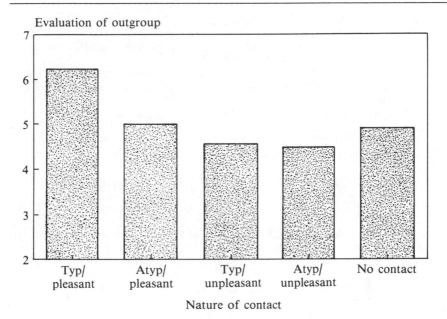

*Figure 2*  Evaluation of an outgroup after contact with a typical or atypical outgroup
member who behaved in either a pleasant or unpleasant manner
*Source*: Adapted from Wilder, 1984, Table 1

## CONCLUSION

In this chapter several theories of prejudice and intergroup conflict have been
reviewed. It is clear that while each theory contributes to our understanding
of these phenomena, there are, nevertheless, important limitations to each.
It would thus appear that a complete understanding of prejudice and intergroup conflict requires multiple perspectives including those that focus on the
individual, those that focus on the group, and those that focus on the relations between groups in society. It is also clear from this review that only
under very specific conditions can we hope to eradicate prejudice and conflict. Such an important undertaking will undoubtedly require the continued
cooperation of specialists from diverse fields of endeavour.

## FURTHER READING

Allport, G. W. (1954). *The nature of prejudice*. Reading, MA: Addison-Wesley.
Brown, R. J. (1988). *Group processes: Dynamics within and between groups*. Oxford:
Basil Blackwell.
Dovidio, J. F., & Gaertner, S. L. (Eds) (1986). *Prejudice, discrimination and racism*.
Orlando, FL: Academic Press.
Hamilton, D. L. (Ed.) (1981). *Cognitive processes in stereotyping and intergroup
behavior*. New York: Lawrence Erlbaum.

## REFERENCES

Abeles, R. P. (1976). Relative deprivation, rising expectations and black militancy. *Journal of Social Issues*, *32*, 119–137.

Abrams, D., & Hogg, M. A. (1988). Comments on the motivational status of self-esteem in social identity and intergroup discrimination. *European Journal of Social Psychology*, *18*, 317–334.

Adorno, T. W., Frenkel-Brunswick, E., Levinson, D. J., & Sanford, R. N. (1950). *The authoritarian personality*. New York: Harper.

Allport, G. W. (1954). *The nature of prejudice*. Reading, MA: Addison-Wesley.

Amir, Y. (1969). Contact hypothesis in ethnic relations. *Psychological Bulletin*, *71*, 319–342.

Aronson, E., Blaney, N., Stephan, C., Sikes, J., & Snapp, M. (1978). *The jig-saw classroom*. London: Sage.

Berkowitz, L. (1962). *Aggression. A social psychological analysis*. New York: McGraw-Hill.

Berry, J. W., Kalin, R., & Taylor, D. M. (1977). *Multiculturalism and ethnic attitudes in Canada*. Ottawa: Supply and Services Canada.

Billig, M. G. (1976). *Social psychology and intergroup relations*. London: Academic Press.

Blake, R. R., & Mouton, J. S. (1962). Overevaluation of own group's product in intergroup competition. *Journal of Abnormal and Social Psychology*, *64*, 237–238.

Brewer, M. B. (1979). In-group bias in the minimal intergroup situation: A cognitive-motivational analysis. *Psychological Bulletin*, *86*, 307–324.

Brewer, M. B., & Campbell, D. T. (1976). *Ethnocentrism and intergroup attitudes. East African evidence*. New York: Sage.

Brewer, M. B., & Miller, N. (1984). Beyond the contact hypothesis: Theoretical perspectives on desegregation. In N. Miller & M. B. Brewer (Eds) *Groups in contact. The psychology of desegregation* (pp. 281–302). Orlando, FL: Academic Press.

Brown, R. (1965). *Social psychology*. New York: Macmillan.

Brown, R. J. (1978). Divided we fall: An analysis of relations between sections of a factory work-force. In H. Tajfel (Ed.) *Differentiation between social groups. Studies in the social psychology of intergroup relations* (pp. 395–429). London: Academic Press.

Brown, R. J. (1984). The role of similarity in intergroup relations. In H. Tajfel (Ed.) *The social dimension: European developments in social psychology* (pp. 603–623). Cambridge: Cambridge University Press.

Brown, R. J., & Abrams, D. (1986). The effects of intergroup similarity and goal interdependence on intergroup attitudes and task performance. *Journal of Experimental Social Psychology*, *22*, 78–92.

Brown, R. J., & Turner, J. C. (1981). Interpersonal and intergroup behaviour. In J. C. Turner & H. Giles (Eds) *Intergroup behaviour* (pp. 33–65). Oxford: Basil Blackwell.

Brown, R. J., & Wade, G. S. (1987). Superordinate goals and intergroup behaviour: The effects of role ambiguity and status on intergroup attitudes and task performance. *European Journal of Social Psychology*, *17*, 131–142.

Campbell, A. (1971). *White attitudes towards black people*. Ann Arbor, MI: Institute for Social Research.

Chapman, L. J., & Chapman, J. P. (1967). Genesis of popular but erroneous diagnostic observations. *Journal of Abnormal Psychology*, *72*, 193–204.

Clark, K. B., & Clark, M. P. (1947). Racial identification and preference in Negro children. In T. M. Newcomb & E. L. Hartley (Eds) *Readings in social psychology* (pp. 169–178). New York: Holt, Rinehart & Winston.

Crosby, F., Bromley, S., & Saxe, L. (1980). Recent unobtrusive studies of black and white discrimination and prejudice: A literature review. *Psychological Bulletin, 87*, 546–563.

Devine, P. (1989). Stereotypes and prejudice: Their automatic and controlled components. *Journal of Personality and Social Psychology, 56*, 5–18.

Diab, L. N. (1970). A study of intragroup and intergroup relations among experimentally produced small groups. *Genetic Psychology Monographs, 82*, 49–82.

Diehl, M. (1988). Social identity and minimal groups: The effects of interpersonal and intergroup attitudinal similarity on intergroup discrimination. *British Journal of Social Psychology, 27*, 289–300.

Doise, W., Deschamps, J.-C., & Meyer, G. (1978). The accentuation of intra-category similarities. In H. Tajfel (Ed.) *Differentiation between social groups. Studies in the social psychology of intergroup relations* (pp. 159–168). London: Academic Press.

Dollard, J., Doob, L. W., Miller, N. E., Mowrer, O. H., & Sears, R. R. (1939). *Frustration and aggression*, New Haven, CT: Yale University Press.

Festinger, L. (1954). A theory of social comparison processes. *Human Relations, 7*, 117–140.

Gaertner, S. L., & Dovidio, J. F. (1986). The aversive form of racism. In J. F. Dovidio & S. L. Gaertner (Eds) *Prejudice, discrimination and racism* (pp. 61–89). Orlando, FL: Academic Press.

Hamilton, D. L. (1981). Illusory correlation as a basis for stereotyping. In D. L. Hamilton (Ed.) *Cognitive processes in stereotyping and intergroup behaviour* (pp. 115–144). New York: Lawrence Erlbaum.

Hamilton, D. L., & Gifford, R. K. (1976). Illusory correlation in interpersonal perception: A cognitive basis of stereotypic judgements. *Journal of Experimental Social Psychology, 12*, 392–407.

Hewstone, M. R. C., & Brown, R. J. (1986). Contact is not enough: An intergroup perspective on the contact hypothesis. In M. R. C. Hewstone & R. J. Brown (Eds) *Contact and conflict in intergroup encounters* (pp. 1–44). Oxford: Basil Blackwell.

Hinkle, S., & Brown, R. (1990). Intergroup comparisons and social identity: Some links and lacunae. In D. Abrams & M. Hogg (Eds) *Social identity theory. Constructive and critical advances* (pp. 48–70). Hemel Hempstead: Harvester-Wheatsheaf.

Holland, C., & Sears, R. R. (1940). Minor studies in aggression: VI. Correlation of lynchings with economic indices. *Journal of Psychology, 9*, 301–310.

Howard, J. W., & Rothbart, M. (1980). Social categorization and memory for ingroup and outgroup behavior. *Journal of Personality and Social Psychology, 38*, 301–310.

Insko, C. A., Nacoste, R. W., & Moe, I. L. (1983). Belief congruence and racial discrimination: Review of the evidence and critical evaluation. *European Journal of Social Psychology, 13*, 153–174.

Jones, E. E., Wood, G. C., & Quattrone, G. A. (1981). Perceived variability of personal characteristics in ingroups and outgroups: The role of knowledge and evaluation. *Personality and Social Psychology Bulletin, 7*, 523–528.

Miller, N., & Brewer, M. B. (Eds) (1984). *Groups in contact. The psychology of desegregation*. New York: Academic Press.

Miller, N., Brewer, M. B., & Edwards, K. (1985). Cooperative interaction in desegregated settings: A laboratory analogue. *Journal of Social Issues, 41*, 63–79.

Miller, N. E., & Bugelski, R. (1948). Minor studies in aggression: The influence of frustrations imposed by the ingroup on attitudes toward outgroups. *Journal of Psychology*, *25*, 437–442.

Mullen, B., Brown, R., & Smith, C. (1992). Ingroup bias as a function of salience, relevance, and status: An integration. *European Journal of Social Psychology*, *22*, 103–122.

Oakes, P. J., & Turner, J. C. (1980). Social categorization and intergroup behaviour: Does minimal intergroup discrimination make social identity more positive? *European Journal of Social Psychology*, *10*, 295–302.

Pettigrew, T. F. (1958). Personality and sociocultural factors in intergroup attitudes: A cross-national comparison. *Journal of Conflict Resolution*, *2*, 29–42.

Quattrone, G. A. (1986). On the perception of a group's variability. In S. Worchel & W. Austin (Eds) *The social psychology of intergroup relations* (2nd edn, pp. 25–48), Chicago, IL: Nelson Hall.

Rabbie, J. M., & Horwitz, M. (1969). Arousal of ingroup–outgroup bias by a chance win or loss. *Journal of Personality and Social Psychology*, *13*, 269–277.

Rokeach, M. (Ed.) (1960). *The open and closed mind*. New York: Basic Books.

Rokeach, M., Smith, P. W., & Evans, R. I. (1960). Two kinds of prejudice or one? In M. Rokeach (Ed.) *The open and closed mind* (pp. 132–168). New York: Basic Books.

Rothbart, M., & Park, B. (1986). On the confirmability and disconfirmability of trait concepts. *Journal of Personality and Social Psychology*, *50*, 131–142.

Runciman, W. G. (1966). *Relative deprivation and social justice*. London: Routledge & Kegan Paul.

Schofield, J. W. (1986). Black–white contact in desegregated schools. In M. Hewstone & R. J. Brown (Eds) *Contact and conflict in intergroup encounters* (pp. 79–92). Oxford: Basil Blackwell.

Schwarzwald, J., & Amir, Y. (1984). Interethnic relations and education: An Israeli perspective. In N. Miller & M. Brewer (Eds) *Groups in contact. The psychology of desegregation* (pp. 53–76). Orlando, FL: Academic Press.

Sherif, M. (1966). *Group conflict and co-operation*. London: Routledge & Kegan Paul.

Simon, B., & Brown, R. J. (1987). Perceived intragroup homogeneity in minority-majority contexts. *Journal of Personality and Social Psychology*, *53*, 703–711.

Slavin, R. E. (1983). When does cooperative learning increase student achievement? *Psychological Bulletin*, *94*, 429–445.

Tajfel, H. (1959). The anchoring effects of value in a scale of judgements. *British Journal of Psychology*, *50*, 294–304.

Tajfel, H. (Ed.) (1978). *Differentiation between social groups. Studies in the social psychology of intergroup relations*. London: Academic Press.

Tajfel, H., & Turner, J. C. (1986). The social identity theory of intergroup behavior. In S Worchel & W. Austin (Eds) *Psychology of intergroup relations* (pp. 7–24). Chicago: Nelson-Hall.

Tajfel, H., & Wilkes, A. L. (1963). Classification and quantitative judgement. *British Journal of Psychology*, *54*, 101–114.

Tajfel, H., Flament, C., Billig, M. G., & Bundy, R. P. (1971). Social categorization and intergroup behaviour. *European Journal of Social Psychology*, *1*, 149–178.

Vanneman, R. D., & Pettigrew, T. F. (1972). Race and relative deprivation in the urban United States. *Race*, *13*, 461–486.

Walker, L., & Mann, L. (1987). Unemployment, relative deprivation, and social protest. *Personality and Social Psychology Bulletin*, *13*, 275–283.

Wilder, D. A. (1984). Intergroup contact: The typical member and the exception to the rule. *Journal of Experimental Social Psychology*, *20*, 177–194.

Worchel, S., Andreoli, V. A., & Folger, R. (1977). Intergroup cooperation and intergroup attraction: The effect of previous interaction and outcome of combined effort. *Journal of Experimental Social Psychology*, *13*, 131–140.

# 5

# NON-VERBAL COMMUNICATION

*Peter Bull*

*University of York, England*

*Lesley Frederikson*

*Massey University, New Zealand*

---

| | |
|---|---|
| **The role of non-verbal cues in social interaction**<br>Emotion<br>Body movement and speech<br>Individual differences | Interpersonal relationships<br>**Practical applications of non-verbal communication research**<br>**Further reading**<br>**References** |

---

There is nothing new in the belief that non-verbal communication is more powerful than speech. Alfred Adler (1870–1937), the neo-Freudian analyst, liked to quote an aphorism from the sixteenth-century Protestant reformer Martin Luther "not to watch a person's mouth but his fists". More recent decades have seen the growth of a popular literature which extols the significance and importance of "body language", while at the same time providing an underlying theme in the more sober pursuits of academic research. Within the rubric of such research can be considered investigations of facial expression, eye contact, pupil dilation, posture, gesture, and interpersonal distance. It can refer as well to communication through touch or smell, through various kinds of artifacts such as masks and clothes, or through formalized communication systems such as semaphore. Sometimes, it has also been used to refer to the vocal features of speech, such as intonation, stress, speech rate, accent, and loudness. Because the term "non-verbal" is a definition only by exclusion, the number of features that can be included under this term is virtually limitless.

The term communication also poses problems of definition, particularly with respect to what behaviours can be properly regarded as communicative. Some theorists have argued that all non-verbal behaviour should be regarded as communicative (e.g., Watzlawick, Beavin, & Jackson, 1968). Other theorists have argued that only those behaviours that are intended to be communicative should be regarded as such (e.g., Ekman & Friesen, 1969a). Both these viewpoints were criticized in an important theoretical paper by Wiener, Devoe, Robinson, and Geller (1972), who argued that for non-verbal behaviour to be regarded as non-verbal communication, it needs to be shown that information is both received and transmitted through non-verbal behaviour: in their terminology, that there is both systematic encoding and appropriate decoding.

Wiener et al. (1972) called their article "Nonverbal behaviour and nonverbal communication", and the distinction is important: not all non-verbal behaviour can be regarded as communicative. Communication can be said to occur only when information transmitted through non-verbal behaviour is accurately and appropriately interpreted by the decoder. Wiener et al. also challenge the view that the only non-verbal behaviours that can be regarded as communicative are those that are intended as such. They point out that the intentions of the encoder are irrelevant; it is often difficult to establish exactly what a person does intend to communicate and there is no basis in the behaviours themselves for deciding whether or not they should be regarded as intentional communications.

Indeed, non-verbal communication may take place even against the express intentions of the encoder. For example, Bull (1987) carried out a number of studies of the way in which listener attitudes and emotions are encoded in posture. They showed that boredom is systematically associated with leaning back, dropping the head, supporting the head on one hand and stretching out the legs (see Figure 1). A person in an audience may show these behaviours without any conscious intention to communicate boredom; nevertheless, this may well be the message that the speaker receives! The person in the audience may even try to suppress these tell-tale signs of boredom by trying hard to appear attentive, but still be incapable of suppressing the occasional yawn. To the speaker, the listener may still communicate that he or she is bored by the talk, despite the best intentions not to do so!

It is also our view that communication can occur without conscious awareness, in the sense that neither encoder nor decoder needs to be able to identify the specific non-verbal cues through which a particular message is transmitted. So, for example, people may be left with the feeling that someone was upset or angry without being able to specify exactly what cues were responsible for creating that impression. Indeed, it can be argued that a great deal of non-verbal communication takes this form, and that one task of the researcher is to try and identify more precisely the cues that are responsible for creating such impressions.

This view of communication can be nicely demonstrated from studies of

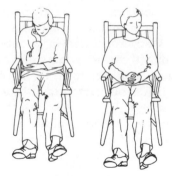

*Figure 1* Postures of boredom
*Source*: Reproduced by permission from Bull, 1983

pupil dilation. Hess and Polt (1960) noticed that on viewing pictures of particular interest, the pupils of their subjects tended to dilate. So, for example, the pupils of women seemed to dilate when seeing a picture of a nude man and a picture of a mother and baby, while the pupils of men dilated when seeing a picture of a nude woman. (In this experiment there was an untested assumption that the subjects were heterosexual; the women's pupils did not dilate as much as the men's to the picture of the nude woman.) In another experiment, Hess (1965) showed a series of pictures to 20 young men, which included two photographs of an attractive young woman. The photos were touched up such that in one case the pupils of the young woman were extra large, and in the other case, extra small (see Figure 2). The pupils of the young men tended to dilate more on seeing the woman with the dilated pupils, although most of the men said the pictures were identical. Hess interpreted these findings as showing that the men found the woman with dilated pupils as more attractive, presumably because they felt she was more attracted to them. Hess (1975) also found that when asked to describe the two photos, they said that the woman with large pupils was "soft", "more feminine", or "pretty", while the same woman with constricted pupils was

80

*Figure 2* Photographs of a woman with dilated and constricted pupils
*Source*: Hess, 1965

described as being "hard", "selfish", or "cold". One of the interesting features of these studies is that none of the students seemed to be aware of the differences in pupil size; nevertheless, these differences appeared to have significant effects on the way in which the woman in the photograph was perceived. Another important feature of pupil dilation is that it is a response of the autonomic nervous system, and hence not under direct voluntary control; in that sense, it cannot be said to be an intentional form of communication (unless you apply belladonna to the eyes or dim the lights!).

But if people communicate unintended messages without awareness through pupil dilation, what is it that is being communicated? Hess (1965) proposed that the pupils dilate in response to stimuli we find attractive, and actually constrict in response to stimuli we find unattractive (the aversion-constriction hypothesis). In fact, this claim has proved to be extremely controversial. Other studies suggest that the pupils simply dilate in arousal, whether that arousal is positive or negative. For example, in one experiment by White and Maltzman (1978), the pupil sizes of students were measured while they were listening to passages read from a novel. One passage was intended to be erotic, another to be neutral, the third passage was an unpleasant description of a lynching mutilation. The authors found an immediate dilation at the beginning of each passage, with the erotic and mutilation passages maintaining pupil dilation for about 60 seconds. Thus, it seems that when aroused, the pupil dilates, although there is no intention to communicate, nor are people necessarily aware of pupil dilation.

## THE ROLE OF NON-VERBAL CUES IN SOCIAL INTERACTION

Non-verbal cues can be said to communicate information about emotion, speech, individual differences, and interpersonal relationships; their significance also needs to be considered in specific social contexts (Bull, 1983).

### Emotion

Particular importance is commonly ascribed to non-verbal cues in the communication of emotion, stemming from the observations of Charles Darwin (1872), who argued that the facial expressions of emotion constitute part of an innate, adaptive, physiological response. In fact, this view has proved to be extremely controversial. Its most explicit rejection came from Birdwhistell (1971), who described how he was initially influenced by Darwin's views, but came to recognize how both the incidence and meaning of, say, smiling might vary between different social groups. Birdwhistell reached the conclusion that "charts of smile frequency were not going to be very reliable as maps for the location of happy Americans". He rejected the view that smiles directly express underlying physiological states, arguing instead that meaning can be understood only within a particular social context.

Later research has provided support for Darwin's observations, although none of the evidence is conclusive. There are cross-cultural studies (e.g., Ekman, Friesen, & Ellsworth, 1972) which show that facial expressions associated with six emotions (happiness, sadness, anger, fear, disgust, surprise) are decoded in the same way by members of both literate and pre-literate cultures. However, Russell (1991) has pointed out that the language used to describe emotion is by no means universal: neither the words for so-called basic emotions such as anger and sadness, nor even the word for emotion itself is found in every culture. He goes on to argue that experiments such as Ekman's, in which people are asked to identify facial expressions from a limited range of emotion categories, may well overestimate universality, because they obscure subtle and significant differences between cultures in the way in which they describe emotion. Moreover, even if one accepts the existence of universals in decoding, it is only necessary to hypothesize that whatever is responsible for common facial expressions is constant for all humankind: inheritance is one such factor, but learning experiences common to all humankind could equally well be another.

A second source of evidence comes from the study of children born deaf and blind. The ethologist Eibl-Eibesfeldt (1973) filmed a number of such children and claimed that they showed the same kinds of basic facial expressions in appropriate situational contexts as do non-handicapped children. Again, a likely explanation for these observations is that such expressions are inherited, but it is still possible that they may be learned through some form of behaviour shaping. Finally, Oster and Ekman (1977) have shown that all but one of the discrete muscle actions visible in the adult can be identified in newborn infants, both full-term and premature. Again, however, this does not prove that the association of particular facial expressions with particular emotions is innate. Smiling can be called a universal gesture in the sense that it is an expression that human beings are universally capable of producing, but this does not mean that it is innately associated with the emotion of happiness, nor that it has a universal meaning.

Thus, although the evidence is consistent with the view that certain facial expressions of emotion are innate, it is by no means conclusive. The rival positions have been neatly reconciled in what Ekman (1972) called his neuro-cultural model of emotional expression. He proposed that there are at least six fundamental emotions with innate expressions which can be modified through the learning of what he calls display rules; display rules refer to norms governing the expression of emotions in different contexts and may take the form of attenuation, amplification, substitution, or concealment of particular expressions. Ekman and Friesen (1986) also provided evidence for a seventh universal facial expression of contempt.

An experiment carried out by Ekman on cross-cultural differences clearly illustrates the use of this model. Ekman, Friesen, and Malmstrom (in Ekman et al., 1972) showed groups of Americans and Japanese a neutral and a stress-inducing film. They saw both films on their own, but their facial expressions were videotaped without their awareness. Both groups differed in their response to the neutral and stress films, but their facial expressions were highly similar. After seeing the stress film, a member of their own culture entered the room and conducted an interview about their experience. The Japanese appeared to engage in substitution by showing happy faces when interviewed by Japanese interviewers, whereas the Americans typically did not conceal signs of negative feelings when they talked with their American interviewer. The experiment nicely supports informal accounts of Japanese culture, where there is said to be a taboo governing the expression of negative emotions in public. The experiment also suggests that the fundamental emotional expressions were shown when the subjects watched the films on their own, but that culturally learned display rules came into operation when interviewed by a member of their own culture.

The neuro-cultural model of emotional expression has important implications for the significance we ascribe to facial expression in the communication of emotion. If there are at least seven innate expressions, then this would suggest that they constitute a particularly important means of communicating information about emotion. However, Ekman and Friesen also point out that we can learn control of our facial expressions through concealment, substitution, amplifications or attenuation. How then can we distinguish between expressions that are posed or spontaneous, between expressions that are faked or genuine? Ekman and Friesen (1982) suggest a number of ways in which spontaneous and false smiles can be distinguished.

In a genuinely felt smile, three action units are involved: raising the corners of the lips, raising the cheeks which may produce crows-feet wrinkles, and raising the lower eyelid. In a false or posed smile, the second and third action units may not be involved. They also suggest that timing may be a cue to posed smiles. A false smile may appear too early or too late. The apex of the smile may be too long — felt smiles seldom last more than 4 seconds. Onset may be too short, giving an abrupt appearance to the smile.

Another clue to the genuineness of an expression is its symmetry. Skinner and Mullen (1991) have published a meta-analysis of 14 studies of asymmetry, in which the authors investigated whether posed expressions are more asymmetrical than spontaneous expressions. Skinner and Mullen criticize earlier research for failing to make a distinction between emotional and neutral posed expressions. They conclude that the effect of asymmetry is much more pronounced for posed emotional expressions, which suggests that asymmetry may indeed be a useful cue in detecting insincere or deceitful expressions. Further cues to deception may come from what Ekman and Friesen call "non-verbal leakage" whereby information about deception is revealed more through body movement than facial expression. They argue that because of the greater repertoire of facial movement, people may be more careful to control their facial movements when trying to deceive others and hence are more likely to give themselves away inadvertently through bodily movements.

The proposal that facial expressions of emotion may be both innate and learned has important implications for the significance that we ascribe to facial expression in the communication of emotion. For example, it means that no simple answer is possible to the question of the relative importance of different cues in communicating information about emotion, since it may depend on whether we are discussing deliberate or spontaneous expressions. In terms of spontaneous expression, it still seems likely that the face constitutes the prime non-verbal source of information about emotion. Facial muscle changes are rapid, the face is usually clearly visible, and there are at least six universal expressions probably innately associated with different emotions. Conversely, the eyes and the pupils lack the same variety of movement as the face and are also less easily discernible. It has yet to be shown that pupil dilation or gaze enables us to distinguish between different emotions; instead, they probably convey information about intensity of emotion rather than the nature of emotion as such (Bull, 1983, pp. 2–9, 43–46). The evidence on posture and gesture is much less clear-cut; it is possible to distinguish between different emotions and attitudes on the basis of posture alone (Bull, 1987).

## Body movement and speech

The central importance of non-verbal cues in the communication of emotion has led some writers to regard body movement as an alternative system to speech, offering a more reliable indicator of people's true feelings. This has been especially true of the popular literature on "body language", in which it seems to be suggested that it represents a kind of "royal road to the unconscious", providing a vital source of information about people's "real" feelings and attitudes. For example, Fast (1970) maintains that body language conveys an emotional message to the outside world that is more reliable than the spoken word: "if the spoken language is stripped away and the only communication left is body language, the truth will find some way of poking through" (Fast, 1970, p. 92).

One particular danger of this viewpoint is that it neglects the extent to which speech and body movement complement each other in communication; indeed, it may be the case that incidence in which non-verbal communication conflicts with speech are the exception rather than the rule. For example, Condon and Ogston (1966) described from a frame-by-frame analysis how the body of the speaker moves closely in time with his or her speech, a phenomenon which they called self-synchrony. Condon and Ogston's observations were not simply confined to hand gestures; it was movements of all parts of the body that they found to be closely synchronized with speech. At the same time, it does not appear to be the case that every bodily movement is related to discourse. Freedman and Hoffman (1967) found in a study of psychotherapy sessions that it was essentially non-contact hand movements (movements that do not involve touching the body) that were judged as related to speech. In a quite different context (that of political speech-making), Bull (1987) also found that it was primarily non-contact rather than contact hand movements that were related to vocal stress. In fact, non-verbal behaviour has been shown to be related to speech in terms of syntax (Lindenfeld, 1971), vocal stress (Pittenger, Hockett, and Danehy, 1960) and meaning (e.g., Scheflen, 1964).

If non-verbal behaviour is so clearly related to speech, what functions does it serve? Ekman and Friesen (1969a) distinguished three types of functions, which they termed emblems, illustrators, and regulators. The term "emblem" refers to those non-verbal acts that have a direct verbal translation, such as nodding the head when meaning "Yes", or shaking the head when meaning "No". Their function is communicative and explicitly recognized as such. Emblems are generally assumed to be specific to particular cultures or occupations, but there do appear to be pan-cultural emblems such as the "eyebrow flash", where a person raises the eyebrows for about one-sixth of a second as a greeting; Eibl-Eibesfeldt (1972) claims to have observed this in a wide number of differing cultures. Morris, Collett, Marsh, and O'Shaughnessy (1979) mapped the geographical distribution of 20 emblems across western and southern Europe and the Mediterranean. Their findings showed that some emblems were specific to one culture. In Italy, for example, pressing and rotating a straightened forefinger against the cheek

*Figure 3*  The cheek-screw
*Source*: Based on a photograph in Morris, Collett, Marsh, and Shaughnessy, 1979. Reproduced
by permission

(sometimes referred to as the cheek-screw) is a gesture of praise; it is, however, little known elsewhere in Europe (see Figure 3).

The meaning of other emblems varies between cultures. A gesture that Morris et al. (1979) call the ring, where the thumb and forefinger touch to form a circle, means in Britain that something is good, in parts of France that something is worthless, while in Sardinia it is an obscene sexual insult (see Figure 4)!

Ekman and Friesen (1969a) argue that the particular importance of

*Figure 4*  The ring
*Source*: Based on a photograph in Morris et al., 1979. Reproduced by permission

emblems stems from the fact that they are often used when speech is difficult or impossible, and hence function as an alternative system to speech. So, for example, the police officer directing traffic on points duty can be said to be using emblems in a situation where speech is not possible. A number of the emblems described by Morris et al. (1979) are insults; the advantage of insulting people at a distance is presumably that it is more difficult for the insulted person to retaliate!

Regulators are movements that are assumed to guide and control the flow of conversation, for example, in the way in which people exchange speaking turns. The most intensive set of studies of turn-taking have been carried out by Duncan and his associates (e.g., Duncan & Fiske, 1985). Duncan found that attempts by the listener to take over the turn could be essentially eliminated by the speaker continuing to gesture; Duncan called this the attempt-suppressing signal. Duncan's observations also showed that ceasing to gesture was one of five turn-yielding cues, signals that offer a speaking turn to the other person. Duncan maintained that the effect of these five cues is additive: his observations showed a linear relationship between the number of turn-yielding cues displayed and a smooth switch between speakers. The other cues were the completion of a grammatical clause, a rise or fall in pitch at the end of a clause, a drawl on the final syllable, and the use of stereotyped expressions such as "you know".

Illustrators are movements that are directly tied to speech; it is maintained that they facilitate communication by amplifying and elaborating the verbal content of the message. Whether illustrators do in fact facilitate communication was tested in an experiment by Rogers (1978). Rogers prepared a silent film of various actions being performed, such as a car making a series of turns, or a tennis ball bouncing into a corner. Observers were asked to view these actions and to describe them to another person who was unable to see the film. These descriptions were videotaped and shown to a second group of observers either with sound and vision, sound only, or in a modified audio-visual condition where the contrast was reduced to obliterate facial information and hence prevent lip-reading. Comprehension was found to be significantly better in the modified audio-visual condition than in the audio condition only, thus suggesting that illustrators do facilitate speech comprehension independently of the information obtained from lip-reading.

Ekman and Friesen's (1969a) threefold distinction into emblems, illustrators, and regulators is useful in that it serves to highlight some of the different functions of gesture in relation to speech. However, a major implication of their typology is that gesture is essentially secondary to speech, either serving as a substitute form of communication when speech is difficult or impossible, or serving to support the spoken message. An alternative view stems from Kendon (1985), who points out that gesture as a silent, visual mode of expression has very different properties from those of speech, and consequently that it is suitable for a different range of communication tasks.

In fact, not only is gesture a visual means of communication, but also it is a highly visible means of communication, especially in comparison to facial expression or eye contact. Hence, gesture may be of particular value to an orator who is physically separated from the audience, such that other aspects of non-verbal communication may not be easily discernible (e.g., Bull, 1987). Again, gesture is extremely useful when seeking to attract someone's attention. Heath (1986) showed in a very interesting analysis of medical consultations that when the (male) doctor's attention was focused on his notes, patients would use more flamboyant gestures as a means of attracting his attention. In this context, gesture has the additional advantage of indirectness as well as visibility, avoiding the need to ask for attention from a higher-status figure like a doctor. This introduces another feature of gesture as a communication system, which is its lack of precision. In certain contexts this can be advantageous where something is too delicate to be put into words.

Not only is gesture a highly visible form of communication, but also there are differences in visibility between different forms of body movement. Scheflen (e.g., 1964) proposed that different sizes of movement are used to indicate structural units of differing importance in conversation. For example, he observed that American speakers change the position of their head and eyes every few sentences. Each of these shifts marks the end of a structural unit, which Scheflen calls a "point", because it corresponds roughly to making a point in a discussion. A sequence of several points go to make up a "position", which corresponds roughly to a point of view that a person may take in conversation. This is a much larger unit of speech and is indicated by a much larger body movement, typically by a gross postural shift involving at least half the body.

The value of emphasizing the distinctive properties of gesture is that it enables us to get a clearer sense of its distinctive role in communication. In fact, Kendon (1985) maintains that gesture is as fundamental as speech for the representation of meaning, that it is separate, in principle equal with speech, joined with speech only because it is used simultaneously for the same purpose. This is consistent with studies on language production, for example, McNeill (1985) has proposed that gestures and speech are part of the same psychological structure and share a common computational stage. The principal evidence for this, McNeill argues, is as follows. Gestures occur primarily during speech. They have semantic and pragmatic functions that parallel those of speech. They are synchronized with linguistic units in speech. They dissolve together with speech in aphasia. They develop together with speech in children.

Thus, gesture should be seen not as an alternative to speech, but as an additional resource, as part of a multichannel system of communication, which allows the skilled speaker further options through which to convey meaning.

## Individual differences

Not only do non-verbal cues encode information about individual differences, but also there are individual differences concerning the extent to which people may transmit information through non-verbal cues: some people may transmit a great deal of information through non-verbal cues, others relatively little (Bull, 1985). For example, Hall (1979) reviewed twenty-six studies in which comparisons were made of sex differences in encoding: nine showed a significant gender difference, eight of which showed that women were clearer encoders. Hence, in this sense women can be seen as more expressive, that is, they transmit more information through non-verbal cues. Men and women also differ in the non-verbal behaviour they use. A review of the literature by Hall (1984) showed a number of consistent non-verbal sex differences. Women both smile more and gaze more at other people; they prefer closer interpersonal distances and are approached more closely than men; they also use smaller and less open body movements and positions. Given that people can make quite subtle judgements about the sex-role attitudes of others on the basis of their non-verbal behaviour alone (Lippa, 1978), it can be argued that such behaviours can be used as a code for communicating information about masculinity and femininity (Bull, 1985). Thus, not only do people differ in the extent to which they transmit information through non-verbal cues, but also the non-verbal cues they do employ may encode significant information about aspects of personality such as sex-role attitudes.

Individual differences in decoding constitute a second important theoretical issue. A number of studies have been carried out to investigate whether groups differ in their decoding ability, whether, for example, women are superior to men in this respect, or whether psychiatric patients are disadvantaged in comparison to the normal population. The importance of these findings is that although non-verbal cues may encode information about, say, emotion, speech, or individual differences, such information may not always be accurately decoded; if certain groups of people fail to decode non-verbal cues appropriately, then the significance of those cues as a form of communication must inevitably vary according to the sensitivity of the decoders.

Hall (1978) reviewed 75 studies of sex differences in decoding non-verbal cues. The majority of these studies made use of posed expressions, in which the decoders' task was to guess what emotions the actor was trying to convey. There were also studies of spontaneous expressions, in which encoders watched films or slides and the decoders' task was to guess from the non-verbal expressions which films or slides the encoders were watching. Of the 75 studies reviewed by Hall, 24 showed a significant sex difference, 23 of which were in favour of women – a proportion that is statistically highly significant. The sex of the encoders does not make any difference: women are better decoders whether they are judging men or other women. Sex differences in decoding are also unaffected by age. Girls are better decoders than boys, just as women are better decoders than men, and it makes no difference whether the encoder is a child or an adult. Subsequently, Hall (1984) analysed a further 50 studies of decoding: 11 of these showed a significant sex difference, 10 of which were in favour of women.

Smith, Archer, and Costanzo (1991) showed a further interesting sex difference in non-verbal cues. They used a test called the Interpersonal Perception Task, which poses questions about videotaped sequences of naturalistic behaviour; each question has an objectively correct answer. They found that, just as with previous research, men performed significantly worse on the task than did women. However, when they were asked to estimate the number of questions they had answered correctly, the men's estimates were significantly higher than the women's. This would suggest not only that women are better at decoding non-verbal cues, but also that either men overestimate their performance, or women underestimate their performance, or both.

### Interpersonal relationships

Non-verbal behaviour varies as a function of the relationships between people. A number of experiments have been carried out in which observers are asked to make judgements about the identity of an unseen conversational partner on the basis of viewing the non-verbal behaviour of one of the conversationalists alone. For example, studies by Abramovitch (e.g., Abramovitch, 1977) have shown that even very young children are capable of accurately discerning the relationship between people from non-verbal cues alone. Benjamin and Creider (1975) showed that adult observers were able to perform this task successfully in terms of the age, sex, and acquaintanceship of the unseen conversational partner. From an analysis of the videotapes, they also identified certain differences in facial expression according to the type of the relationship. When adults talked to children, their muscle tonus was low, the skin beneath the eyes and over the cheek bones hanging loosely down except during broad smiles, whereas when adults talked to other adults, their skin was bunched and raised. There also appear to be significant differences in the activity rate between same-age and different-age conversations, conversations between people of the same age appearing to be much more animated. The significance of these studies is not only that non-verbal behaviour varies according to the nature of the relationship, but also that decoders can utilize such information to discern the relationship between people in terms of sex, age, and acquaintanceship.

One cue that appears to be of particular significance in interpersonal relationships is postural congruence. This refers to people imitating one another's postures, which Scheflen (1964) claimed indicates similarity in views or roles in a group; conversely, non-congruence of posture is used to indicate marked divergences in attitude or status. In a study based on

Scheflen's observations, Charny (1966) analysed a film of a psychotherapy session. Postures were categorized as congruent or non-congruent; a further distinction was made between mirror-image congruent postures, where one person's left side is equivalent to the other's right, and identical postures, where right matches right and left matches left (see Figure 5). Charny found that as the interview progressed, there was a significant trend towards spending more time in mirror-congruent postures. He also found that the speech associated with these postures was more positive, concluding that they may be taken as indicative of rapport or relatedness. Identical postures rarely occurred during the session, so were not included in the final analysis.

LaFrance investigated whether postural congruence is related to rapport in American college seminars. In one study, LaFrance and Broadbent (1976) found a significant positive correlation between mirror-congruent postures and a questionnaire intended to measure rapport, a significant negative correlation between non-congruent postures and rapport, and no significant relationship between identical postures and rapport. In a second study, LaFrance (1979) measured posture and rapport during the first week (time 1) and the final week (time 2) of a six-week seminar course to investigate the

*Figure 5*  Postural congruence. The pair in the foreground are showing identical postures, the pair in the background mirror-image postures
*Source*: Reproduced by permission from Bull, 1983

probable direction of causality between mirror-congruent postures and rapport, using a method of statistical analysis known as the cross-lag panel technique. The results suggested that it is postural congruence that may be influential in establishing rapport.

Thus, a number of encoding studies of postural congruence do show that it is related to rapport. Another way of investigating the phenomenon is to see how postural congruence is decoded. Trout and Rosenfeld (1980) set up an experiment to investigate the perception of postural congruency in simulated therapist–client interactions. They arranged for two male US graduate students to play the roles of therapist and client, and to adopt either mirror-congruent or non-congruent postures; there was no soundtrack, and the faces were blocked out of the tape. The results showed that the mirror-congruent postures were rated as indicating significantly more rapport than the non-congruent postures. Thus, given the evidence from studies of both encoding and decoding, it appears that postural congruence does communicate rapport.

Non-verbal communication also plays an important part in courtship: Grammer (1990) proposed that its function is both to enhance attractiveness and to show interest and availability. In fact, the very vagueness of non-verbal communication can be an advantage. Whereas direct verbal invitations require an explicit response, non-verbal invitations are not so binding and can be withdrawn, refused, or denied without giving offence or causing loss of self-esteem. Grammer has looked in detail at the non-verbal cues associated with sexual interest. He observed opposite-sex pairs of strangers in conversation, and correlated their non-verbal behaviour during laughter with ratings of sexual interest. He found that interest was significantly associated with a number of distinct body movements and postures but that it did not correlate with laughter. Postures of individual body parts can be combined to produce a total body posture which indicates an overall level of interest. In fact, Grammer found that the effect is additive: the more of the high-interest postures that are present the higher the level of expressed interest. This allows "fine-tuning" in signalling interest through various combinations of high and low interest postures.

Non-verbal behaviour can thus be used to identify the type of relationship between people, and it is also important within relationships. Studies of postural congruence have shown that the configuration of postures between people is important, while Grammer's (1990) study highlights the meaning of distinct signals communicated between members of the opposite sex.

## PRACTICAL APPLICATIONS OF NON-VERBAL COMMUNI-CATION RESEARCH

There is no doubt that the systematic study of non-verbal behaviour does have considerable practical significance. According to the social skills model, social behaviour can be seen as a kind of motor skill involving the same kinds of processes as, for example, driving a car or playing a game of tennis (Argyle & Kendon, 1967). The advantage of this approach is that we can apply ideas and concepts developed in the study of motor skills to the study of social interaction.

One major implication of this model is that, if social behaviour is seen as a skill, then it is possible for people to improve their performance as with any other skill. This learning might take the form of a systematic course in social skills training, or it might be the case that simply reading a book on non-verbal communication may be sufficient to improve the quality of a person's social relationships (as is typically claimed in the popular literature on "body language"). One of the best known forms of social skills training is assertiveness training (e.g., Rakos, 1991). In fact, the two terms have sometimes been used interchangeably, although it is now recognized that assertiveness refers to a more limited set of interpersonal skills. Both these forms of training include specific instruction in non-verbal behaviour especially in the areas of encoding and decoding.

Social skills training has been used with a wide variety of populations for a wide variety of different problems. For example, it has been used as a way of improving people's ability to handle conversations, to improve their perceptiveness of others, and to improve people's performance in job interviews. It has also been used as a form of therapy for psychiatric patients experiencing a range of different problems. In addition, it has been used as a form of professional training with, for example, teachers, doctors, nurses, and police officers. In fact, the principles of social skills training can be applied to virtually any situation involving interpersonal communication. Wright (1989) cites the case of a disabled law student who was confined to a wheelchair and was also unable to produce a normal range of manual gestures. Her oral presentations were criticised for not appearing sufficiently aggressive, so she was encouraged (within the limits of her disability) to develop a range of head and shoulder movements and to utilise assertive pauses in the presentation to emphasize important points. The resulting communication was viewed as more assertive and better suited for the student's purpose.

One possible criticism of social skills training is the extent to which it may embody the prejudices and preconceptions of the social skills trainer. However, with advances in non-verbal communication research, it is now possible to use objective tests as a means of instruction, such as Costanzo and Archer's (1989) Interpersonal Perception Task (IPT) referred to earlier. This is an objective test of non-verbal perceptiveness, based on naturally occurring sequences of behaviour. Decoders are shown 30 brief scenes, each of which is paired with a multiple-choice question with two or three options. In every case, the answer to the question is completely objective. For example, two of the scenes show a woman talking on the telephone. In each scene, the decoders are asked to identify to whom she is talking. In the first scene (see Figure 6) the choice is between her mother, a female friend she has known for many years, or a male friend she has known for many years. In the second scene (see Figure 7) the choice is between her mother, a female friend, or her boyfriend.

The IPT has been used by Costanzo and Archer (1991) as a means of teaching about non-verbal communication; they found that a group instructed in this way performed significantly better than another group attending traditional lectures. The real value of the IPT is that it can be used not only to objectively assess skill in decoding but also as a means of improving non-verbal perceptiveness. However, perceptiveness is only one aspect of social skill; in terms of the social skills model, the selective perception of cues has to be transformed through central translation process into effective motor responses. Thus, it is perfectly possible for someone to be highly perceptive without being able to translate that perceptiveness into appropriate social behaviour. In this sense, we also need objective tests of encoding, which will be useful both as a means of assessing encoding skill and as a means of improving encoding performance.

Despite these reservations, the significance of advances in non-verbal communication research should not be underestimated. Studies since the 1960s have unquestionably demonstrated the importance of non-verbal behaviour in interpersonal communication; as a consequence, our concept of what constitutes communication has been substantially enhanced, while a more

*Figure 6* Who is the woman talking to on the telephone?
*Source*: Reproduced by permission from Archer and Costanzo, 1988

*Figure 7*   Who is the woman talking to on the telephone?
*Source*: Reproduced by permission from Archer and Costanzo, 1988

profound and sophisticated understanding has been acquired of the processes
and practice of social interaction.

## FURTHER READING

Argyle, M. (1988). *Bodily communication* (2nd edn). London: Methuen.
Bull, P. E. (1983). *Body movement and interpersonal communication*. Chichester:
Wiley.
Ekman, P., & Friesen, W. V. (1975). *Unmasking the Face*. Englewood Cliffs, NJ:
Prentice-Hall.
Rakos, R. F. (1991). *Assertive Behavior*. London: Routledge.
Smith, H. J., Archer, D., & Costanzo, M. (1991). "Just a hunch": Accuracy and
awareness in person perception. *Journal of Nonverbal Behavior*, *15*, 3–18.

## REFERENCES

Abramovitch, R. (1977). Children's recognition of situational aspects of facial expres-
sion. *Child Development*, *48*, 459–463.
Archer, D., & Costanzo, M. (1988). *The Interpersonal Perception Task (IPT)*.
(Available from University of California Extension Center for Media and
Independent Learning, 2176 Shattuck Avenue, Berkeley, CA, 94704, USA.
Argyle, M., & Kendon, A. (1967). The experimental analysis of social performance.
In L. Berkowitz (Ed.) *Advances in Experimental Social Psychology* (vol. 3,
pp. 55–97). New York: Academic Press.
Benjamin, G. R., & Creider, C. A. (1975). Social distinctions in non-verbal behavior.
*Semiotica*, *14*, 52–60.

Birdwhistell, R. L. (1971). *Kinesics and context*. London: Allen Lane, The Penguin Press.

Bull, P. E. (1983). *Body movement and interpersonal communication*. Chichester: Wiley.

Bull, P. E. (1985). Individual differences in non-verbal communication. In B. D. Kirkcaldy (Ed.) *Individual differences in movement* (pp. 231–245). Lancaster: Medical and Technical Press.

Bull, P. E. (1987). *Posture and gesture*. Oxford: Pergamon.

Charny, E. J. (1966). Psychosomatic manifestations of rapport in psychotherapy. *Psychosomatic Medicine, 28*, 305–315.

Condon, W. S., & Ogston, W. D. (1966). Sound film analysis of normal and pathological behavior patterns. *Journal of Nervous and Mental Diseases, 143*, 338–347.

Costanzo, M., & Archer, D. (1989). Interpreting the expressive behavior of others: The Interpersonal Perception Task (IPT). *Journal of Nonverbal Behavior, 13*, 225–245.

Costanzo, M., & Archer, D. (1991). A method for teaching about verbal and non-verbal communication. *Teaching of Psychology, 18*, 223–226.

Darwin, C. (1872). *The expression of emotions in man and animals*. London: Murray.

Duncan, S., & Fiske, D. W. (1977). *Face-to-face interaction: Research and theory*. Hillsdale, NJ: Lawrence Erlbaum.

Duncan, S., & Fiske, D. W. (1985). *Interaction structure and strategy*. New York: Cambridge University Press.

Eibl-Eibesfeldt, I. (1972). Similarities and differences between cultures in expressive movements. In R. A. Hinde (Ed.) *Non-verbal communication* (pp. 297–311). Cambridge: Cambridge University Press.

Eibl-Eibesfeldt, I. (1973). The expressive behaviour of the deaf-and-blind born. In M. Von Cranach & I. Vine (Eds) *Social communication and movement* (pp. 163–194). London: Academic Press.

Ekman, P. (1972). Universal and cultural differences in facial expressions of emotion. In J. R. Cole (Ed.) *Nebraska symposium on motivation*, 1971 (pp. 207–283). Lincoln, NE: University of Nebraska Press.

Ekman, P., & Friesen, W. V. (1969a). The repertoire of nonverbal behavior: Categories, origins, usage and coding. *Semiotica, 1*, 49–98.

Ekman, P., & Friesen, W. V. (1969b) Non-verbal leakage and clues to deception. *Psychiatry, 32*, 88–106.

Ekman, P., & Friesen, W. V. (1982). Felt, false and miserable smiles. *Journal of Nonverbal Behavior, 6*, 238–252.

Ekman, P., & Friesen, W. V. (1986). A new pan-cultural facial expression of emotion. *Motivation and Emotion, 10*, 159–168.

Ekman, P., Friesen, W. V., & Ellsworth, P. (1972). *Emotion in the human face: Guidelines for research and an integration of findings*. New York: Pergamon.

Fast, J. (1970). *Body language*. New York: Evans.

Freedman, N., & Hoffman, S. P. (1967). Kinetic behavior in altered clinical states: Approach to objective analysis of motor behavior during clinical interviews. *Perceptual and Motor Skills, 24*, 527–539.

Grammer, K. (1990). Strangers meet: Laughter and nonverbal signs of interest in opposite-sex encounters. *Journal of Nonverbal Behavior, 14*, 209–236.

Hall, J. A. (1978). Gender effects in decoding non-verbal cues. *Psychological Bulletin, 85*, 845–857.

Hall, J. A. (1979). Gender, gender roles and non-verbal communication skills. In R. Rosenthal (Ed.) *Skill in non-verbal communication: Individual differences* (pp. 32–67). Cambridge, MA: Oelgeschlager, Gunn & Hain.

Hall, J. A. (1984). *Nonverbal sex differences: Communication accuracy and expressive style*. Baltimore, MD: Johns Hopkins University Press.

Heath, C. (1986). *Body movement and speech in medical interaction*. Cambridge: Cambridge University Press.

Hess, E. H. (1965). Attitude and pupil size. *Scientific American, 212*, 46–54.

Hess, E. H. (1975). The role of pupil size in communication. *Scientific American, 233*, 110–119.

Hess, E. H., & Polt, J. M. (1960). Pupil size as related to interest value of visual stimuli. *Science, 132*, 349–350.

Kendon, A. (1985). Some uses of gesture. In O. Tannen & M. Saville-Troike (Eds) *Perspectives on silence* (pp. 215–234). Norwood, NJ: Ablex.

LaFrance, M. (1979). Non-verbal synchrony and rapport: Analysis by the cross-lag panel technique. *Social Psychology Quarterly, 42*, 66–70.

LaFrance, M., & Broadbent, M. (1976). Group rapport: Posture sharing as a non-verbal indicator. *Group and Organisation Studies, 1*, 328–333.

Lindenfeld, J. (1971). Verbal and non-verbal elements in discourse. *Semiotica, 3*, 223–233.

Lippa, R. (1978). The naive perception of masculinity-femininity on the basis of expressive cues. *Journal of Research in Personality, 12*, 1–14.

McNeill, D. (1985). So you think gestures are nonverbal? *Psychological Review, 92*, 350–371.

Morris, D., Collett, P., Marsh, P., & O'Shaughnessy, M. (1979). *Gestures: Their origins and distribution*. London: Cape.

Oster, H., & Ekman, P. (1977). Facial behaviour in child development. In A. Collins (Ed.) *Minnesota symposium on child psychology vol. II* (pp. 231–276). Minneapolis, MN: Minnesota University Press.

Pittenger, R. E., Hockett, C. F., & Danehy, J. J. (1960). *The first five minutes: A sample of microscopic interview analysis*. Ithaca, NY: Martineau.

Rakos, R. F. (1991). *Assertive behavior*. London: Routledge.

Rogers, W. T. (1978). The contribution of kinesic illustrators toward the comprehension of verbal behaviour within utterances. *Human Comunication Research, 5*, 54–62.

Russell, J. A. (1991). Culture and the categorization of emotions. *Psychological Bulletin, 110*, 426–450.

Scheflen, A. E. (1964). The significance of posture in communication systems. *Psychiatry, 27*, 316–331.

Skinner, M., & Mullen, B. (1991). Facial asymmetry in emotional expression: A meta-analysis of research. *British Journal of Social Psychology, 30*, 113–124.

Smith, H. J., Archer, D., & Costanzo, M. (1991). "Just a hunch": Accuracy and awareness in person perception. *Journal of Nonverbal Behavior, 15*, 3–18.

Trout, D. L., & Rosenfeld, H. M. (1980). The effect of postural lean and body congruence on the judgment of psychotherapeutic rapport. *Journal of Nonverbal Behavior, 4*, 176–190.

Watzlawick, P., Beavin, J. H., & Jackson, D. D. (1968). *Pragmatics of human communication*. London: Faber & Faber.

White, G. L., & Maltzman, I. (1978). Pupillary activity while listening to verbal passages. *Journal of Research in Personality, 12*, 361–369.

Wiener, M., Devoe, S., Robinson, S., & Geller, J. (1972). Nonverbal behavior and nonverbal communication. *Psychological Review, 79*, 185–214.

Wright, G. (1989). The miscommunication of nonverbal behavior of persons with physical disabilities and the implications for vocational assessment. *Vocational Evaluation and Work Adjustment Bulletin*, Winter, 147–150.

# GLOSSARY

This glossary is confined to a selection of frequently used terms that merit explanation or comment. Its informal definitions are intended as practical guides to meanings and usages. The entries are arranged alphabetically, word by word, and numerals are positioned as though they were spelled out.

**accommodation 1.** in Piaget's theory of cognitive development, the type of adaptation in which old cognitive schemata are modified or new ones formed in order to absorb information that can neither be ignored nor adapted through assimilation into the existing network of knowledge, beliefs, and expectations. **2.** In vision, modification of the shape of the eye's lens to focus on objects at different distances. **3.** In social psychology, the modification of behaviour in response to social pressure or group norms, as for example in conformity (q.v.).

**affect** any subjectively experienced feeling state or emotion (q.v.), such as euphoria, anger, or sadness.

**altruism** in social psychology and sociobiology, behaviour that benefits another individual or individuals in terms of safety, monetary or other advantages, or chances of survival and reproduction, at some cost to the benefactor. *See also* reciprocal altruism.

**attitude** a fairly stable evaluative response towards a person, object, activity, or abstract concept, comprising a cognitive component (positive or negative perceptions and beliefs), an emotional component (positive or negative feelings), and a behavioural component (positive or negative response tendencies).

**attribution** in social psychology, the ascription of motives, attitudes, traits, or other characteristics to oneself or another person, especially in order to explain or understand that person's behaviour. *See also* fundamental attribution error.

**audience effect** *see under* social facilitation.

**authoritarian personality** a personality (q.v.) type strongly disposed to racial and other forms of prejudice (q.v.), first identified in 1950, characterized by rigid adherence to conventional middle-class values, submissive, uncritical attitudes towards authority figures, aggressive, punitive attitudes towards people who violate conventional norms, avoidance of anything subjective or tender-minded, an inclination to superstition, preoccupation with strong-weak dichotomies, cynical distrust of humanity in general, a tendency towards projection of unconscious emotions and impulses, and preoccupation with the sexual activities of other people.

**autonomic nervous system** a subdivision of the nervous system (q.v.) that regulates (autonomously) the internal organs and glands. It is divided into the sympathetic nervous system and the parasympathetic nervous system (qq.v.).

**availability heuristic** a heuristic (q.v.) in which the frequency or probability of an

99

event is judged by the number of instances of it that can readily be brought to mind and that are thus cognitively available. It can generate biased or incorrect conclusions, as when people are asked whether the English language contains more words beginning with the letter *r* or more with *r* as the third letter. Most people find it easier to think of instances of the former than the latter and so conclude wrongly that there are more words beginning with *r*.

**central nervous system (CNS)** in human beings and other vertebrates, the brain and spinal cord.

**classical (Pavlovian) conditioning** the process, first described by the Nobel Prize-winning Russian physiologist Ivan Petrovich Pavlov, sometimes called respondent conditioning, by which an initially neutral stimulus acquires the capacity to elicit a response through association with a stimulus that naturally elicits that response. *Cf.* operant conditioning.

**co-action effect** *see under* social facilitation.

**cognition** from the Latin *cognoscere*, to know, attention, thinking, problem-solving, remembering, and all other mental processes that fall under the general heading of information processing.

**cognitive dissonance** a motivating state of tension first identified by the American psychologist Leon Festinger that occurs when a person simultaneously holds two cognitions – items of knowledge, attitudes, or beliefs – that are psychologically inconsistent. A person in a state of cognitive dissonance is motivated to eliminate or reduce the dissonance, and this often involves changes in attitudes (q.v.) or beliefs.

**conditioning** *see under* classical (Pavlovian) conditioning, operant conditioning.

**conformity** the modification of attitudes, opinions, or behaviour in response to social pressure from group members or prevailing social norms.

**construct validity** in psychometrics (q.v.), the validity (q.v.) of a test established by investigating whether it yields the results predicted by the theory underlying the trait that the test purports to measure.

**content validity** in psychometrics (q.v.), the validity (q.v.) of a test estimated via a systematic examination of the items of which it is composed.

**correlation** in statistics, the relationship between two variables such that high scores on one tend to go with high scores on the other or (in the case of negative correlation) such that high scores on one tend to go with low scores on the other. The usual index of correlation, called the product-moment correlation coefficient and symbolized by $r$, ranges from 1.00 for perfect positive correlation, through zero for uncorrelated variables, to $-1.00$ for perfect negative correlation.

**correlational study** a non-experimental type of research design in which patterns of correlations (q.v.) are analysed.

**criterion validity** in psychometrics (q.v.), the validity (q.v.) of a test determined by applying it to groups of people who are known to differ on the trait that the test purports to measure.

**de-individuation** the loss of one's sense of individuality, personal accountability, and self-monitoring that as occurs in some crowd situations when individual behaviour gives way to mob action. *See also* diffusion of responsibility.

**diffusion of responsibility** the reduced sense of personal responsibility and individual accountability experienced in some circumstances by members of a group, often leading to behaviour untypical of any of the group members when alone. *See also* de-individuation, social loafing.

**DSM-IV** the common name of the fourth edition of the *Diagnostic and Statistical*

*Manual of Mental Disorders* of the American Psychiatric Association, published in 1994, replacing DSM-III-R, the revised version of the third edition published in 1987, containing the most authoritative classification and definitions of mental disorders.

**emotion** from the Latin *e*, away, *movere*, to move, any evaluative, affective, intentional, short-term psychological state. *See also* expressive behaviour, primary emotions.

**encoding** the conversion of information into a code suitable for transmission as a signal, as when a person converts a felt emotion into a facial expression or gesture that conveys non-verbal information to any onlooker who can decode the message.

**equivalent-form reliability** a measure of the reliability (q.v.) of a psychological test based on the correlation (q.v.) between scores obtained on two equivalent versions of the test; if the test measures reliably, and if the equivalent forms really are equivalent, the correlation should be high. *Cf.* split-half reliability, test-retest reliability.

**expectancy-value model** an influential theory of the relationship between behaviour and attitudes, put forward by Fishbein and Ajzen in 1975, according to which behaviour is an additive linear function of the individual's attitude towards the behaviour in question and subjective norm (perception of the extent to which others think the behaviour should be performed). The individual's attitude towards the behaviour, in turn, is a multiplicative function of the individual's beliefs about the consequences of the behaviour and evaluation of each consequence.

**expressive behaviour** behaviour, especially facial expressions and other forms of non-verbal behaviour, that expresses emotional states or attitudes. *See also* emotion, primary emotions, non-verbal communication.

**factor analysis** a statistical technique for analysing the correlations between a large number of variables in order to reduce them to a smaller number of underlying dimensions, called factors, in a manner analogous to the way in which all spectral colours can be reduced to combinations of just three primary colours.

**fundamental attribution error** a pervasive tendency to overestimate the importance of internal, dispositional factors, and to underestimate external, situational factors, when explaining the causes of other people's behaviour. *See also* attribution.

**game theory** a branch of mathematics, with applications in social psychology, behavioural ecology, and sociobiology, devoted to the analysis of interdependent decision-making in any situation in which two or more decision makers, called players, each choose between two or more options, called strategies, and the outcome depends on the choices of all players.

**group polarization** a tendency for group decisions to be more extreme, in the direction of the predominant group opinion, than the individual opinions of the group members. In the special case of decisions involving risk, if the predominant group opinion favours a risky decision, the phenomenon is called the risky shift.

**halo effect** a tendency to overestimate on many traits a person who is outstanding on one trait.

**heuristic** from the Greek *heuriskein*, to discover, any of a number of methods of solving complex problems by means of rough-and-ready rules of thumb. *See also* availability heuristic.

**instrumental conditioning** *see* operant conditioning.

**learning** the relatively permanent change in behaviour that occurs as a result of experience. *See also* classical (Pavlovian) conditioning, operant conditioning.

**locus of control** in personality theory and social psychology, the perceived source of control over one's behaviour, on a scale from internal to external.

**mental disorder** according to DSM-IV (q.v.), a psychological or behavioural syndrome or pattern associated with distress (a painful symptom), disability (impairment in one or more areas of functioning), and a significantly increased risk of death, pain, disability, or an important loss of freedom, occurring not merely as a predictable response to a disturbing life-event.

**motivation** the motive forces responsible for the initiation, persistence, direction, and vigour of goal-directed behaviour.

**need for achievement (achievement motivation)** a social form of motivation (q.v.) involving a competitive drive to meet standards of excellence, traditionally measured with a projective test such as the Thematic Apperception Test (TAT) (q.v.). *Cf*. need for affiliation.

**need for affiliation** a social form of motivation (q.v.) involving a drive to associate and interact with other people. *Cf*. need for achievement (achievement motivation).

**negative reinforcement** reinforcement (q.v.) that results from the removal rather than the presentation of the reinforcer (which, by implication, is an aversive or punishing negative reinforcer). *Cf*. positive reinforcement.

**nervous system** *see under* autonomic nervous system, central nervous system (CNS), parasympathetic nervous system, sympathetic nervous system.

**non-verbal communication** the collective name for all forms of communication apart from spoken or written language, including the communicative effects of vocal quality, facial expression, postures, and gestures.

**observational learning** *see* vicarious learning.

**operant conditioning** a type of learning, sometimes called instrumental conditioning, which focuses on the process by which behaviour changes as a result of its consequences, in particular the way in which an individual's behavioural responses become more or less frequent as a consequence of reinforcement (q.v.). *Cf*. classical (Pavlovian) conditioning.

**parasympathetic nervous system** one of the two major divisions of the autonomic nervous system; its general function is to conserve metabolic energy. *Cf*. *sympathetic nervous system*.

**Pavlovian conditioning** *see under* classical (Pavlovian) conditioning.

**perception** the processing of sensory information from the receptors (q.v.). *Cf*. sensation.

**personality** from the Latin *persona*, mask, the sum total of all the behavioural and mental characteristics that distinguish an individual from others.

**positive reinforcement** a process of reinforcement (q.v.) in which the relative frequency of the response is increased by the presentation of a reinforcer with rewarding properties. *Cf*. negative reinforcement.

**prejudice** literally pre-judgement, that is, a preconception or a premature opinion based on insufficient evidence; more specifically, a negative attitude (q.v.) towards a whole category of people, especially a minority group within society. *See also* authoritarian personality.

**primary emotions** according to Paul Ekman, the six emotions of happiness, sadness, disgust, fear, anger, and surprise, so-called partly because their associated facial expressions are evidently innate: many appear soon after birth, even in infants born blind and deaf, and have been found to be similar in all cultures that have been studied. *See also* emotion, expressive behaviour, non-verbal communication.

**projective tests** psychological tests designed to tap deep-lying psychological processes, usually consisting of weakly structured or ambiguous stimulus materials on to which the perceiver is assumed to project ideas, which may be unconscious. *See also* Rorschach test, Thematic Apperception Test (TAT).

**prosocial behaviour** any form of socially cooperative behaviour, including especially altruism (q.v.) and helping behaviour.

**psychoanalysis** a theory of mental structure and function and a method of psychotherapy based on the writings of Sigmund Freud and his followers, focusing primarily on unconscious mental processes and the various defence mechanisms that people use to repress them.

**psychology** from the Greek *psyche*, mind, *logos*, study, the study of the nature, functions, and phenomena of behaviour and mental experience. psychometrics from the Greek *psyche*, mind, *metron*, measure, mental testing, including IQ, ability, and aptitude testing and the use of psychological tests for measuring interests, attitudes, and personality traits and for diagnosing mental disorders.

**receptor** a sense organ or structure that is sensitive to a specific form of physical energy and that transmits neural information to other parts of the nervous system (q.v.).

**reciprocal altruism** altruism (q.v.) or helping behaviour whose performance or continuation is conditional on the recipient behaving altruistically or helpfully in return.

**reinforcement** in learning theory, the strengthening of the bond between a stimulus and a response (qq.v.) or anything that increases the relative frequency of a response. *See also* negative reinforcement, positive reinforcement, reinforcer.

**reinforcer** any stimulus or event that increases the relative frequency of a response during the process of reinforcement (q.v.).

**reliability** in psychometrics (q.v.), the consistency and stability with which a measuring instrument performs its function. *See also* equivalent-form reliability, split-half reliability, test-retest reliability. *Cf.* validity.

**respondent conditioning** *see* classical (Pavlovian) conditioning.

**response** any behavioural or glandular activity of a person or an animal, especially as a reaction to a stimulus (q.v.).

**responsibility diffusion** *see* diffusion of responsibility.

**risky shift** *See under* group polarization.

**Rorschach test** a projective test (q.v.) named after the Swiss psychiatrist Hermann Rorschach consisting of 10 cards on which are printed bilaterally symmetrical inkblots to which the testee responds by describing what the inkblots look like or what they bring to mind.

**sensation** acquisition by the body's internal and external sense organs or receptors (q.v.) of 'raw' information. *Cf.* perception.

**social cognition** from the Latin *socius*, a companion, + cognition, the study of how people perceive and understand all aspects of their social environments, especially the behaviour of other people and themselves. *See also* attribution.

**social facilitation** the enhancing effect on behaviour of the mere presence of others, either as passive spectators (audience effect) or as co-actors (co-action effect).

**social learning** learning that occurs through observation of the behaviour of others, called models, together with imitation, and vicarious learning (q.v.).

**social loafing** the tendency for individual effort to diminish in group task situations, partly as a consequence of diffusion of responsibility (q.v.).

**social motivation** any form of motivation (q.v.) associated with social behaviour, manifested in such phenomena as need for achievement (achievement motivation), need for affiliation, social facilitation, and social loafing (qq.v.).

**social psychology** from the Latin *socius*, a companion, + psychology, a branch of psychology concerned with the study of social behaviour and the mental experience of individuals in social contexts.

**sociogram** a pictorial representation derived from sociometry (q.v.) of the social relationships in a group.

**sociometry** from the Latin *socius*, a companion and the Greek *metron*, measure, the measurement of social relationships, especially friendship patterns, within groups. *See also* sociogram.

**split-half reliability** a measure of the reliability (q.v.), more specifically the consistency, of a psychological test determined by calculating the correlation (q.v.) between scores obtained on half the test items, arbitrarily chosen, with scores obtained on the other half; if the test measures consistently, the correlation should be high. *Cf*. equivalent-form reliability, test-retest reliability.

**stereotype** from the Greek *stereos*, solid, *tupos*, type, an over-simplified, biased, and above all inflexible conception of a social group. The word was originally used in the printing trade for a solid metallic plate which was difficult to alter once cast.

**stimulus** (pl. stimuli) any objectively discernable event capable of evoking a response (q.v.) in an organism.

**subjects** from the Latin *sub*, under, *jacere*, to throw, people or other organisms whose behaviour or mental experience is investigated in psychological research.

**sympathetic nervous system** one of the two major divisions of the autonomic nervous system; it is concerned with general activation, and it mobilizes the body's reaction to stress or perceived danger. *Cf*. parasympathetic nervous system.

**test-retest reliability** a measure of the reliability (q.v.) of a psychological test, more specifically its stability, determined by calculating the correlation (q.v.) between scores obtained by a group of subjects on the test on two separate occasions; if the test measures stably, and if the psychological characteristic being measured is stable over time, the correlation should be high. *Cf*. equivalent-form reliability, split-half reliability.

**Thematic Apperception Test (TAT)** a projective test (q.v.) based on a series of somewhat ambiguous pictures about which the testee is asked to tell imaginative stories.

**unconscious** occurring without awareness or intention; in psychoanalysis (q.v.), the name for the part of the mind containing instincts, impulses, images, and ideas of which one is not normally aware.

**validity** from the Latin *validus*, strong, in psychometrics (q.v.), the degree to which a measuring instrument measures what it purports to measure. *See also* construct validity, content validity, criterion validity. *Cf*. reliability.

**vicarious learning** from the Latin *vicarius*, substituted, learning that occurs through the observation of others' behaviour and its consequences, also called observational learning. *See also* social learning.

# INDEX